Sacred Geometry: Design Your Life with Cosmic Principles

How can the tenets of an ancient art help you gain insight into your life's path and purpose today? In *Techniques for Geometric Transformation*, John Michael Greer shows you how to use the forgotten wisdom of sacred geometry as a tool for expanded perception; a way to develop awareness of the hidden patterns of reality that shape your everyday life.

Easy to learn and use, the Sacred Geometry Oracle provides clear, insightful, and accurate readings about past, present, and future events. It emphasizes possibility, and the ability to choose the future you want.

Once, ancient builders used sacred geometry as a tool to design temples and pyramids in accordance with cosmic patterns and universal truths. With the knowledge you gain from this Oracle, you can design your own life with the same sort of grace, power, and connection to the cosmos.

About the Author

John Michael Greer has been a student and practitioner of Hermetic magic and Western esoteric spirituality since 1975. The author of several books, including *Natural Magic: Potions and Powers from the Magical Garden* and *Earth Divination, Earth Magic: A Practical Guide to Geomancy*, and numerous articles on Western magical traditions, he is also an initiated Druid of the Order of Bards Ovates and Druids (OBOD), a student of geomancy and sacred geometry, a Certified Tarot Master, and an active member of two magical lodges. He lives in Seattle.

To Write to the Author

If you wish to contact the author or would like more information about this book, please write to the author in care of Llewellyn Worldwide and we will forward your request. Both the author and publisher appreciate hearing from you and learning of your enjoyment of this book and how it has helped you. Llewellyn Worldwide cannot guarantee that every letter written to the author can be answered, but all will be forwarded. Please write to:

John Michael Greer
℅ Llewellyn Worldwide
P.O. Box 64383, Dept. 0-7387-0051-7
St. Paul, MN 55164-0383, U.S.A.
Please enclose a self-addressed stamped envelope for reply,
or $1.00 to cover costs. If outside U.S.A., enclose
international postal reply coupon.

Many of Llewellyn's authors have websites with additional information and resources. For more information, please visit our website:

http://www.llewellyn.com

TECHNIQUES
FOR
GEOMETRIC
TRANSFORMATION

JOHN MICHAEL GREER

2002
Llewellyn Publications
St. Paul, Minnesota 55164-0383, U.S.A.

First Edition
First Printing, 2002

Card and cover design by Gavin Dayton Duffy
Editing and book design by Rebecca Zins

Library of Congress Cataloging-in-Publication Data
Greer, John Michael.
    Techniques for geometric transformation / John Michael Greer.—1st ed.
       p. cm.
    Includes bibliographical references (p.) and index.
    ISBN 0-7387-0051-7
    1. Fortune-telling by cards. 2. Geometry—Miscellanea. I. Title.

BF1878 .G74 2002
133.3'33—dc21

                            2001046292

Llewellyn Worldwide does not participate in, endorse, or have any authority or responsibility concerning private business transactions between our authors and the public. All mail addressed to the author is forwarded but the publisher cannot, unless specifically instructed by the author, give out an address or phone number.

Any Internet references contained in this work are current at publication time, but the publisher cannot guarantee that a specific location will continue to be maintained. Please refer to the publisher's website for links to authors' websites and other sources.

Llewellyn Publications
A Division of Llewellyn Worldwide, Ltd.
P.O. Box 64383, Dept. 0-7387-0051-7
St. Paul, MN 55164-0383, U.S.A.
www.llewellyn.com

 Printed in the United States of America on recycled paper

Contents

The Third Circle

Introduction to the Sacred Geometry Oracle

We live in a time of great transitions. After three centuries in which the Western world has been dominated by the ideology of science, more and more people are taking a hard look at the legacy of the Scientific Revolution, with its dream of a world totally subjected to human reason and its promise of limitless power through technology. The dream and the promise measure up poorly against the hard realities of a spiritually empty, esthetically debased, culturally impoverished, and environmentally devastated world.

In the last fifty years, in response to these concerns, teachings concerning mysticism, magic, divination, and inner development have come out of the shadows to play an ever more prominent role in modern life. These ancient traditions have proven themselves quite capable of handling the complexities of a postmodern world—more capable, indeed, than many approaches that carry the seal of official scientific approval.

In the modern renaissance of traditional wisdom, though, the ancient art of sacred geometry has played a surprisingly small role. At a time when the basic ideas of traditional wisdom are becoming ever more widely known, when everything from astrology to Zen has a ready and increasingly knowledgeable audience, very few people have even encountered sacred geometry.

Much of the problem is simply a matter of how sacred geometry has been presented in modern times. Memories of boring math classes make the whole idea of sacred geometry seem cold, abstract, and difficult to those who have never experienced it, and getting past this barrier has been a slow and difficult process.

With a few stellar exceptions, too, most of the very small handful of recent books on sacred geometry fall short as useful introductions to the art. On the one hand, these books betray a limited and sometimes inaccurate knowledge of the traditional lore. On the other, many of them have a habit of mixing sacred geometry together with a dizzying assortment of speculations about lost continents, ancient astronauts, conspiracy theories, and the like. While I don't intend to pass judgment on such ideas, or to deny them merit on their own terms, it's fair to say that they don't have much to do with traditional sacred geometry; muddling them together with geometrical studies has caused far more confusion than clarity, and done some damage to sacred geometry's reputation besides.

Despite its importance, then, sacred geometry remains the most neglected of the Western world's wisdom teachings. This is particularly unfortunate at the present time, for it has things to offer that our modern world desperately needs. It was by way of sacred geometry that ancient architects, artists, designers, and builders created structures and works of art that still astonish the viewer by their beauty, their practicality, and their harmonious relationship to their surroundings. It was by way of sacred geometry that the spiritual and the practical sides of life were woven together seamlessly in the everyday environments of city, town, workplace, and home. In an age when our cities are drowned in soulless ugliness, and our lives are surrounded by objects designed for mechanical efficiency without any human qualities whatsoever, the insights of sacred geometry have much to offer us even on a practical level.

Understanding Sacred Geometry

Our culture's forgetfulness of sacred geometry extends so far that many people have never heard of it, and some of those who know the term use it in ways the traditional sacred geometers of the past would hardly recognize. Thus, a few paragraphs on matters of definition may be useful here.

The English word "geometry" comes from the Greek *geometria*, literally "earth measurement" (from *ge*, "earth," and *metron*, "measure"). This points back to the ancient origins of geometry, when the art was used to lay out patterns on the earth in order to measure fields and establish the ground plans for sacred structures.

At that time, all geometry was sacred, for two reasons. On the one hand, the Earth itself was understood as a living and holy being, and those who measured it and patterned it recognized their responsibility as mediators between the Earth and the people. Historically we can find echoes of this attitude in the sacred status of boundary stones, in rituals performed at the founding of a city or the building of a temple, and in many other traditions that have endured from the distant past. This attitude had much to do with the origins of feng shui in China, and of similar systems, far less well-known, in the Western world and elsewhere.

On the other hand, it was recognized early on that geometry itself offered pathways into the subtle realm of meaning and spirit that we call sacred. The play of geometric form obeys laws that unfold from the nature of experienced reality itself, laws that are not subject to human whims or prejudices. Mastery of those laws provided knowledgeable individuals with tools to reshape the world, both on a physical level—for geometry was the foundation of much of ancient architecture and technology—and on subtler levels as well.

Out of this recognition of the sacred possibilities of geometry, an extraordinary tradition of wisdom took shape. It was expressed in many different forms in the cultures that treasured it; the forgotten geometers who planned and built the mighty stone circles of northwestern Europe no doubt understood geometry in very different ways from the temple priests of Egypt, the initiates of the Pythagorean Brotherhood of ancient Greece, the Taoist sages of China, or the master builders of medieval Europe. Their work varied equally; it takes different methods and somewhat different skills to trace out the design of a stone circle, to erect a Gothic cathedral, to work out the proportions of a Renaissance painting, or to teach a new initiate to apply geometrical principles of balance and harmony to his or her own daily life.

Still, a common thread of insight runs through all of these expressions of the sacred geometry tradition. All of them recognized the need to join geometric theory with its expression in practice. All of them knew how to fuse spirit, form, and matter into unity through the practice of their art. All of them recognized that beauty and meaning come from the presence of the living spirit in form and matter, and all of them saw clearly that this comes *through* the creative mind from beyond, not *from* the individual ego and its manipulations.

These insights, however, did not remain central to geometric practice. As societies grew more complex and human activities more specialized, the practical side of geometry grew away from its roots in the living spirit. This was a slow process, and by no means a continuous one. While there are records of purely practical geometry from ancient Egyptian times, there were still times and places thereafter when the practical and spiritual sides of geometry were reunited, giving rise to soaring works of human genius, such as the temples of classical Greece and the Gothic cathedrals of medieval Europe.

Only with the end of the Renaissance and the coming of the Scientific Revolution did the break become total. It's not an accident that the term "sacred geometry" came into being after this point. Only when the main current of geometry in the West lost the last of its connections to the sacred was it necessary to create a new phrase, "sacred geometry," to refer to what all geometry had once been.

We can define sacred geometry, then, as *the art of using geometric forms as a gateway to the knowledge and presence of the living spirit*. If your only contact with geometry has been with the sort that's taught in public schools, in other words, the approach on which the Sacred Geometry Oracle is based may seem pretty strange. The emblems and exercises in this book, and in other books of traditional sacred geometry, have nothing to do with proving theorems or calculating the sides of triangles! Instead, sacred geometry is about opening up the self to the experience of geometric form, recognizing the presence of underlying laws in the play of form, and learning to understand the universe in a different and deeper way.

Geometry was only one of a group of ancient arts with the same broad purpose and approach, and most of the cultures that made use of sacred geometry drew on these other arts as well. In the Western world, from Greek times to the end of the Renaissance, these arts were united as the *quadrivium* or "Four Ways" of arithmetic, geometry, music, and astronomy.

All of these, it has to be remembered, were studied and practiced as sacred disciplines. Nowadays, we might use different names to better communicate what the branches of the quadrivium were about: *numerology*, the spiritual science of number; *sacred geometry*, the spiritual science of form; *harmonics*, which embraces not only the inner dimensions of music, but also the whole realm of relationship and proportion; and *calendrics*, the spiritual science of the cycles of time. All these interact in complex ways; some of those interactions will be explored later on in this book.

The Sacred Geometry Oracle

The book and deck you hold in your hands are an introduction to this ancient tradition, designed to be used as a way of divination—that is, as a means of tapping into the subtle patterns of existence to gain insight into past, present, and future events. Sacred geometry has ancient connections with the realm of prophecy and divination, reaching back to the prehistoric stone circles where priests and priestesses watched the skies for portents.

Turning traditional wisdom into a set of divining cards is not a new idea. An old legend claims that the tarot deck came into being when priests of an ancient civilization sought ways to transmit their spiritual teachings to the future. Whether or not this is historically true, the idea seems worth trying!

The Oracle consists of thirty-three cards, each bearing an important diagram from the lore of traditional sacred geometry. These diagrams have meanings of their own, and those meanings can readily be related to the events and situations of everyday life. When we get to the point, run around in circles, work at cross-purposes, or go off on a tangent, we're already interpreting our lives in geometric terms. The same sort of awareness can be turned to the subtle and communicative designs of sacred geometry, making them into symbols that—like the runes, the cards of the tarot deck, the figures of geomancy, or the hexagrams of the I Ching—serve as a bridge between intuitive awareness and the world of our experience.

The thirty-three cards of the Oracle are divided into three circles of eleven cards each. These circles are stages in a path of initiation, and those who wish to understand the Oracle at a deeper level, through the exercises and meditations included in this book, may find that path opening up before them. Understood in their fullness, the cards are gateways that lead in many directions.

Each of the cards has a name, a number, an image or diagram, a pair of keywords, and a pair of divinatory meanings. The name on each card is the title of the diagram on the card in traditional sacred geometry, and the number is simply a way of putting the cards in their proper numerical order.

The image or diagram on each card is a geometric construction that expresses the essential principle of the card. At one level, this can simply be used as a visual image, as a way of remembering the card, and as an anchor for its meanings. At a deeper level, those who take the time to learn what the construction is and what it represents will find that the diagram itself has much in the way of guidance to offer.

Each card also has two keywords, one upright, one reversed, which are for use in divination. In some card-based oracles, upright cards are given positive meanings, and reversed ones are given negative ones. This sort of approach seems unnecessarily limiting, since every event has its positive and negative sides, and the most difficult experiences often present us with the richest opportunities for growth and healing.

In the Sacred Geometry Oracle, the upright or reversed positions of the cards symbolize situations and events that are more comfortable, on the one hand, or more challenging, on the other, and the keywords reflect this. It's important to keep in mind that a reading with many reversed cards isn't "bad"; it simply means that the querent (the person for whom the reading is done) faces a series of challenges—or, to say the same thing in different words, a series of opportunities.

The divinatory meanings for the cards are given in the following pages, and expand on the upright and reversed keywords in various ways. The meanings are given under two headings. The first focuses on the card as symbol and metaphor, relating the meanings of the card to the traditions of sacred geometry. The second, more practically oriented, gives common ways in which the card may be interpreted in actual divinations. Some people find one way of talking about meanings more useful, some prefer the other. You may find it valuable to refer to both, especially in the early stages of learning to use the Oracle.

It should always be kept in mind that the meanings given here aren't hard and fast rules for interpretation. Rather, they're suggestions and hints meant to spur your own intuitive abilities and guide you to a personal sense of the meaning of each card. Eventually, if you work with the Oracle and pay attention to the messages it gives you, you'll develop your own understanding of the cards, and this is exactly as it should be. Staying rigidly fixated on the literal meaning of the texts that follow is like trying to jump off a diving board and hang onto it at the same time, and the best advice is the same in either case: let go!

The Exercises

Each card also comes with a geometric exercise, which is included in the pages that follow. The prospect of actually doing sacred geometry—rather than just reading about it, thinking about it, or looking at diagrams that make use of it—will fascinate some people and frighten others. For the sake of the latter group, it should be said first off that you don't have to do the exercises in order to use the Oracle for divination.

On the other hand, if you do decide to attempt the exercises, the result will be a much deeper comprehension of the cards, as well as a good basic introduction to the practice of traditional sacred geometry itself. If you intend to study sacred geometry on its own terms, rather than simply using the Oracle for divination, carrying out the exercises is essential. Trying to learn sacred geometry without drawing diagrams in the traditional way is like trying to become a musician without ever picking up an instrument.

The basic toolkit of the geometer consists of a pen or pencil, a straightedge or ruler, and a compass—the geometer's kind, not the sort you use to find out where north is (the sort you probably used in school, with a little yellow pencil that clips to one side, is fine). You can get all of these in the school supplies section of your local drugstore for a few dollars. These three things, along with a supply of unlined paper, will be all you'll need for most of the geometric exercises given here. A few other things will be useful in certain exercises:

- a length of string;
- several pushpins, the sort used to hold things up on bulletin boards;
- graph paper, preferably with small squares (around ¼" works well);
- heavy paper or light poster board;
- clear tape;
- a craft knife, or a sharp pair of scissors.

Armed with these simple and inexpensive tools, you'll be ready to tackle any of the constructions in this book.

Since we live in an age of computers, some readers may want to do the exercises onscreen with a graphics program. While this is one possible way to go about it, it misses much of the point and most of the value that's to be gained by doing the exercises by hand, with real paper and physical tools. The subtle interplay of mind, hand, pen, and paper is an important aspect of the learning process. To be learned on any level but a shallow, intellectual one, the patterns of sacred geometry need to be embodied—literally, made part of your body—by the process of carrying out the exercises of the art. It's by approaching each exercise as a moving meditation, a sacred dance of pen and paper, that the inner reaches of sacred geometry are reached.

This brings up another point, and an important one, about these exercises. It's valuable to do the exercises once, but if you want to go beyond the most basic level of studying sacred geometry, they should be done many times, until the patterns take shape on the paper with practiced ease. The patterns of traditional sacred geometry do not teach all their lessons at once. It takes patience, persistence, and steady work to give those lessons room to unfold within you.

The Meditations

Each of the cards also has a meditation associated with it. Again, as with the geometric exercise, it should be said right at the beginning that you don't need to do the meditations to used the Sacred Geometry Oracle for divination—but again, as with the exercises, those who venture into this phase of the system will be rewarded by deeper insights into the cards, as well as a solid introduction to the practice of Western meditation.

It's not often realized that the Western world has meditation traditions of its own, and that these are different from the systems of India, eastern Asia, and other parts of the world. There are many similarities—the human mind is much the same everywhere—but one central difference.

This lies in the attitudes of these different systems toward the thinking mind. In the East, most systems of meditation teach the student to stop the thinking process altogether, by repeating mantras (special patterns of spoken sound), constructing complex symbolic visualizations, or concentrating on thought-stopping paradoxes such as the koans of Zen.

In Western mystical traditions, by contrast, the approach that's more common is to train and reorient the thinking mind, not merely to shut it down. Ever since the time of Pythagoras, if not before, Western mystics and sages have recognized that the mind need not be the enemy of the spirit if it's brought into harmony with itself, with the larger human self of which it forms a part, and with the cosmos as a whole. *The rational can be a vehicle for the spiritual:* this is the premise (and the promise) of most Western mystical paths, and particularly of those in which sacred geometry has flourished.

In the thirty-three meditations that follow, then, the crucial skill you'll be learning is the ability to think in a meditative way. Like everything else, this takes practice, and you'll find that the more often you do the meditations, the more skill you'll develop in doing this. While the meditations given here are basic ones—the heights of meditation lead far beyond what can usefully be covered in an elementary book like this one—steadfast and regular practice can take you a long way. Don't assume that one session spent on a given meditation, or for that matter ten sessions, will reveal everything that the subject of the meditation has to teach!

There are certain preliminaries that will be used all through the meditations in this book. Start by sitting down and finding a stable, comfortable position. If you want to use one of the cross-legged postures standard in Asian meditative traditions, and have the flexibility to do it comfortably, do so. If not, find a chair with a plain, cushionless seat. Sit far enough forward on it that your back isn't resting against the back of the chair. Your feet should be flat on the floor, and feet and knees should be touching; your thighs should be parallel to the floor, and your lower legs vertical from knee to ankle. Straighten your back without stiffening it, and hold your head upright, as though you were balancing something on it. Your hands should rest palms-down on your thighs, and your elbows should be against your sides. This is the standard Western posture for meditation.

Once you've settled into your position, consciously relax each part of your body, starting with your feet and moving step by step up to the top of your head. Then spend a few minutes paying conscious attention to your breath, breathing in and out slowly, evenly, and fully.

If you wish, a traditional breathing exercise called the Fourfold Breath can be used here. Breathe slowly in while counting mentally from one to four; hold your breath in, while counting from one to four; breathe out, counting from one to four; and hold the breath out, with the lungs empty, while counting from one to four, and repeat. The counts should all be at the same pace, and the breath should be held in or out with the muscles of the chest and diaphragm, not by closing the throat, which can lead to health problems.

After you've paid attention to your breathing for perhaps five minutes, turn your attention to the subject of the meditation. Each of the meditations given in this book will give you specific instructions for how to go on from there. In every case, though, keep your mind focused on the subject, and if it strays—as it will, especially at first— bring it gently back to the subject. When you're done, pay attention to your breathing again for a minute or so to help yourself make the transition back to more ordinary kinds of awareness.

Finally, it's a standard part of the work of meditation to write down a brief description of each practice session immediately after it's over. The date, the time, the length of the session, the subject on which you were meditating, and any results or conclusions you may have reached should be included. A diary or practice journal kept in this way will give you a valuable tool to track your progress over time.

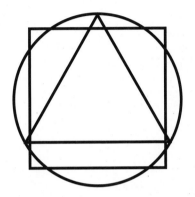

The First Circle

THE UNMARKED CARD

I

POTENTIALITY • HIDDENNESS

I: The Unmarked Card

In ancient times, paper had not yet been invented and writing materials such as parchment and papyrus were expensive. The ancient masters of sacred geometry thus traced out their diagrams on many different kinds of working surfaces. The word *geometry* itself literally means "earth measurement," a reminder that the living earth itself was the original surface on which the patterns of sacred geometry were drawn.

In Greek and Roman times, wax tablets that could be warmed, smoothed, and used again were common. Later, in the age of the great cathedrals, the builders' diagrams were drawn in chalk on wooden tracing boards; "tracing board" remains a common term in some modern traditions of sacred geometry.

Card 1, The Unmarked Card, represents the tracing board or working surface of the sacred geometer, ready for use but not yet marked in any way. What patterns will you draw on it?

Upright Meaning: Potentiality

WHEN IT APPEARS UPRIGHT IN A READING, The Unmarked Card suggests that the situation is entirely open. No points, lines, or patterns have yet been drawn on the tracing board before you, and you can make whatever designs you wish. Do you want to create a simple diagram or a complex one, or plan a cottage, a palace, or a pyramid? It's up to you.

IN PRACTICAL DIVINATION, this card upright usually means that your own choices and actions in the present, rather than legacies of your earlier actions or decisions made by others, will have the most important influence on how matters turn out. It represents a situation in which you are more or less free to do as you wish. Let your dreams soar!

Reversed Meaning: Hiddenness

WHEN IT APPEARS REVERSED IN A READING, The Unmarked Card suggests that the tracing board is not as blank as it appears at first glance. While it looks as though nothing has been decided or determined yet, there are lines and patterns you can't see, and they will have effects on your design that you cannot calculate with the information on hand.

IN PRACTICAL DIVINATION, this card reversed means that there are important things you don't yet know about the situation. Your options may be limited in ways you don't expect—by other people's actions, by the effects of choices you yourself have made at some earlier time, or by other factors you haven't yet recognized. It may be a good time to gather more information before you commit yourself too deeply to any particular plan or project.

Exercise for Card 1

For this exercise, you'll need the usual tools of the sacred geometer mentioned in the Introduction—pen, straightedge, and compass—but you won't actually use any of them! Simply set them down in front of you, along with a piece of blank, unlined paper. Look at the paper, and think about the various patterns you could draw on it with the tools you have. Imagine points, lines, arcs, circles, triangles, squares, and more complex designs as well. Picture them on the paper . . . and then let the images fade, and return your attention to the plain, blank surface of the paper in front of you. Do this for a few minutes at least, and do something else before you go on to any of the other exercises in this book.

The point of this exercise may be clear to you as soon as you do it, or it may not. This actually doesn't matter that much. It's useful to remember that in sacred geometry, as in so much of life, it's more important to *do* things than to understand them intellectually. If you have a strongly visual imagination and pay attention to the instructions, it's possible to do any of the exercises in this book in your head . . . but most of the lessons they have to teach will remain hidden from you unless you actually pick up the tools of sacred geometry and do the exercises right here in the material world.

Meditation for Card 1

For many people nowadays, the sort of emptiness symbolized by Card 1 is something to fear and avoid. Few people can handle as much as five minutes of silence and solitude without becoming bored and uncomfortable. Too often, we turn to the media or to other people to fill up the emptiness, rather than paying attention to the many lessons it has to teach—not to mention wondering what it is about emptiness that frightens us so much.

This is where the practice of meditation becomes so important. In nearly all systems of meditation, one of the central skills to be learned is the ability to handle stillness, silence, and emptiness. It's been said that meditation is one of the most boring activities there is, and this is true—but it's a half-truth, not the whole truth. It's by the practice of meditation that we can learn to pay attention to what is actually going on inside us and around us . . . and that quickly leads to discoveries that are anything but boring. The following meditation is a way to begin this work.

As mentioned in the Introduction, each of the meditations on the cards focuses on a particular subject. For Card 1, the subject is—nothing at all! Once you've finished the opening process outlined earlier, simply let your mind empty itself of thoughts, and do your best to keep it that way.

As soon as you try this, of course, various kinds of mental chatter will spring up to fill the emptiness. Images, ideas, fantasies, worries, things you need to do as soon as the meditation is over and things you should be doing instead of meditating will all come rushing into your awareness. This sort of mental static is one of the constants of meditation, at least in the early stages.

The cure for it is simple . . . though "simple," here as elsewhere in life, is not the same thing as "easy." As soon as you notice that your awareness has strayed away from emptiness, simply bring it back and let the thought go. Odds are you'll have to do it again, and again, and again as you take the first steps toward clarity.

To begin with, five minutes of this meditation is enough. With practice, you'll find yourself achieving a relaxed yet vigilant state of inner clarity, in which your awareness reflects only itself and intruding thoughts don't arise. This state is one of the great gifts of meditation, and you'll want to try to achieve it for a few moments at the start of each of the other meditations in this book, between the period of rhythmic breathing and the time you spend exploring the actual subject of the meditation.

2: The Point

The journey of a thousand miles, it's been well said, begins with a single step. Every human being unfolds like a geometric design from a single point—a fertilized ovum, smaller than the period at the end of this sentence. In one sense, this is the image of the divine in which each of us is made. In the same way, every design in sacred geometry—simple or complex, basic or advanced, abstract or practical—begins with a single point.

Geometrically speaking, the point has neither length, width, nor depth; it is pure existence, without any dimensions or qualities at all.

All we can say about it is that it is, and that everything else depends on it and unfolds from it. Does this sound familiar? In many of the world's spiritual traditions, sages and mystics have pointed out that these same statements are also true of that creative Mystery which, for want of a better word, we may as well call "God."

In the symbolism of sacred geometry, the point corresponds to the concept of unity. Every point is exactly the same as every other point; the only difference is where any given point happens to be located. From ancient times, this has been used as a metaphor for the presence of the divine in the universe.

Upright Meaning: Beginning

WHEN IT APPEARS UPRIGHT IN A READING, The Point suggests that the moment has arrived to make a beginning. Whatever design you intend to make on the tracing board of your life, you need to begin it somewhere, by making the point from which everything else will unfold. If you don't know exactly where the first point should be placed, make your best guess and go ahead.

IN PRACTICAL DIVINATION, this card upright means that it's time to choose what you want to do, and start actually doing it. Daydreams, speculations, worries, and "what-ifs" all have their proper place and time, but that's not here and now. The German poet Goethe's advice is worth taking: "Whatever you can do, or dream you can, begin it. Boldness has genius and power and magic in it. Begin it now!"

Reversed Meaning: Commitment

WHEN IT APPEARS REVERSED IN A READING, The Point suggests that you have already made the first mark on the tracing board before you, and whatever patterns you will be drawing from now on will have to take that initial point into account. The marking of the first point is a transition from freedom to commitment, one that cannot be reversed without starting the entire process again from the beginning.

IN PRACTICAL DIVINATION, this card reversed means that whatever you may have intended, you're already too deeply involved in the situation to be able to back out with any degree of grace or effectiveness. Like it or not, you've committed yourself, and one way or another you are going to have to deal with the results of that commitment.

Exercise for Card 2

As you did with the exercise for Card 1, take the three tools of sacred geometry—the pen, the straightedge, and the compass—and set them down in front of you, along with a sheet of plain, unlined paper. In this exercise, you'll be using only the first of the tools, the pen. The point and the pen are linked symbolically as well as practically; in both senses, the business end of the pen is nothing but a point, a way of marking position in the unbounded, undefined space of the blank tracing board.

Start out by considering the sheet of paper in front of you, as you did in the exercise for Card 1, imagining the different patterns you can bring into being on its blank surface. Then slowly, deliberately, and with intent, make a mark somewhere on the paper: a single dot, as small as you can make it.

Now consider the paper again. Whatever you do with the paper from this time on, that point will play a role. Even if you deliberately draw a pattern that doesn't relate to it at all, it will be there, suggesting connections and relationships by its simple presence. Go ahead and imagine different patterns on the paper, as before, but see how the point you have drawn interacts with them and shapes them.

When you've done this for a few minutes, set the paper aside. Don't throw it out; you'll need it for the next exercise.

Meditation for Card 2

For this meditation, start with the same opening process as before—the stable, balanced position, the step by step relaxation of the body, the period of attention to rhythmic breath, and the deliberate clearing of the mind. Try, as mentioned above, to reach that state of calm watchfulness in which your awareness contains nothing but itself. Then, after a moment or so, move on to the subject of the meditation.

The subject is, simply, the idea of a geometrical point. Start by imagining a point, all alone in an emptiness that extends in every direction without limit. Let this image build up solidly in your mind's eye until you can see the point clearly in the middle of infinite space.

Now think of the point itself as infinitely small, without length or width or depth—pure position, as the old definition has it, without magnitude. Think about the way these two infinities, the infinitely small in the midst of the infinitely vast, mirror each other. Consider any comments that particularly struck you in the discussion of the card above, and see how they relate to the ideas just mentioned.

Turn all this over in your mind in a general way for a time, and then choose some particular train of thought that it sets in motion and follow that as far as it goes, trying to relate each step back to the image of the point in the middle of infinite space. If you find that your thoughts have strayed away from the subject, bring them back to the image, and then try to pick up the train of thought at the point where it derailed, and follow it further. When you've taken it as far as you can, close the meditation in the way described in the Introduction.

3: The Line

Once the first step has been taken, the next one follows. Once a process has been set in motion, it unfolds according to the innate laws of its development, unless some other factor comes into play. In the same way, after the point comes the line.

The line is one of the two basic constructions unfolding from the point, and along with the other—the circle—it gives rise to all other patterns. In geometrical terms, a line can be drawn between any two points, and once drawn it extends to infinity in both directions. It has one dimension, the dimension of length. It has a special relationship with the straightedge, the geometer's tool used to draw lines.

In sacred geometry, the line corresponds to the idea of duality. Partly this is a reflection of the two points that define any given line, but it also suggests the two very different uses that the line has in geometrical work. On the one hand, the line connects; it unites the two points that define it, and extends the relationship between them out to infinity. On the other hand, the line separates; it divides the tracing board or the abstract plane on which it is drawn into two parts. Both these factors are equally important to the line's meaning.

Upright Meaning: Extension

WHEN IT APPEARS UPRIGHT IN A READING, The Line suggests that the point you've already drawn can be connected to another point somewhere else on the tracing board before you. This involves moving beyond the beginning you've already made, and building on the past without being limited by it. Remember that every line reaches out all the way to infinity, no matter how close together lie the two points that define it.

IN PRACTICAL DIVINATION, this card upright means that it's time to proceed with plans and projects you've already set in motion. Where The Point focuses on beginnings, The Line puts emphasis on follow-through. You've already established your starting point; now it's time to choose another point—the one toward which you're aiming—and trace out the line from one to the other.

Reversed Meaning: Separation

WHEN IT APPEARS REVERSED IN A READING, The Line represents a line of separation across the tracing board before you. That line is formed by the beginning you've made and the goals that you've set, and it extends out to infinity in both directions; there's no way around it. Some things will fall on one side, some things on another, and there's not much you will be able to do about that fact. Once the line is traced, separation follows.

IN PRACTICAL DIVINATION, this card reversed means that the changes you've set in motion are going to require you to let go of one or more things in your life. As you extend the line, so must you extend yourself, and that extension may be accompanied by various kinds of growing pains. The most common of these is the pain of having to give up the familiar, safe, comfortable surroundings you've grown used to. When a baby is born, it finds itself thrust out from the comforts of the womb into a cold, strange, and challenging new world. One way or another, this is always the price of growth.

Exercise for Card 3

For this exercise, you'll need your pen and straightedge, and the sheet of paper marked with a single point from the exercise for Card 2. Set the paper before you, consider it, and then mark a second point on the paper, wherever you like. (The only requirement is that it shouldn't be precisely on top of the first point!)

Once you've drawn the second point, take your straightedge and line it up on the two points. If at all possible, the straightedge should extend off the edge of the paper on both sides. With your pen, draw the line that connects the two points, and extend it out to the edge of the paper in both directions. Set the straightedge aside, and consider the line for a few moments; try to see how it unites and separates at the same time.

If you like, repeat this exercise several different times, marking your two points in different places on the paper and extending the lines accordingly. Practice positioning the straightedge so that the line you draw with it goes exactly through the two points; if you don't have much experience with practical geometry or drafting, this will help a good deal with some of the more detailed geometric exercises to come.

Meditation for Card 3

The process for this meditation is exactly the same as the one you used in the meditation for Card 1; the only difference is in the topic.

Start as before, by sitting in a stable position, relaxing your body, paying attention to your breath for a few minutes, and then seeking the state of balanced clarity. Once you've completed these steps, go to the topic, which is the line.

Start by imagining a point in the middle of infinite space, as in the meditation for Card 2. When this image is solidly built up in your mind's eye, imagine another point, some distance away from the first one. Try to hold both points at once in your imagination; be aware of the relationship between them, and the endless space opening up to either side.

Then allow a perfectly straight line to form between the points, connecting them and shooting off in both directions, past the points and toward infinity. Follow the line with your mind's eye in one direction, and then in another, then return to the two points and the line connecting them.

Now think about the line and the points it connects, and allow the image to suggest ideas to you. Make use of any ideas that interested you in the discussion of the card above. Are there parts of your life that remind you of the interaction between the points and the line? What does that interaction look like from the perspective of each of the points? How about from that of the line?

As before, choose one train of thought and follow it as far as you can; if your thoughts stray off the topic, take them back to the image, and then bring them back on track. When you've taken the train of thought as far as it can go, close the meditation as before.

4: The Circle

The line, as we've seen, is one of the two basic constructions of sacred geometry; the circle is the other. Both line and circle start out from the relationship between two points, but do so in radically different ways. Each one is the other's opposite, mathematically as well as symbolically. Where the line connects point to point, and reaches out to infinity in two directions, the circle takes one point as its center and the other one as a measure of distance, keeping them permanently separate, and traces an arc that curves back on itself into unity. Where the line is the source of all growth and expansion, the circle is the source of all containment and limitation.

Some modern ways of thinking treat limitation as though it's always a bad thing, but this is just another example of how far out of touch we sometimes get with the realities of the cosmos. It's worth recalling that in living things, unlimited growth has a special name; we call it "cancer." Limitation and growth, expansion and contraction—both have their necessary place in the dance of life, unfolding step by step in ever more complex relationships out of the creative freedom symbolized by the point.

In another sense, the circle can be seen as the point in an expanded form, since it is made up of all the points at a given distance from its center. For this reason, the circle has often been used as a symbol of spirit or of divine power present in the world. This may seem unrelated to the meanings just given, but most of the time the divine or the spiritual is our name for the furthest limit of our perceptions—"the highest circle of spiralling powers," in Nikos Kazantzakis' phrase.

Upright Meaning: Continuity

WHEN IT APPEARS UPRIGHT IN A READING, The Circle suggests that the patterns you draw at this point in your design should be based on relationships you've already established and boundaries you've already set. In the designs you've already made are the seeds of endless complexity and beauty, and this may be a good time to allow those seeds to germinate, instead of digging them up and planting new ones in their place. Patience and gentle persistence are called for at this stage in the unfolding of things.

IN PRACTICAL DIVINATION, this card upright generally means that it's a good time to pay attention to routine activities, and to turn away from new projects and requests that you extend yourself into unfamiliar territory. It can mean that you're not in a good place to begin new projects; it can also mean that you've already set in motion the patterns that will bring you your heart's desire, and you need to tend to them, rather than neglecting them for something new. Attention to your home and family circle may be a good idea, and in some circumstances it may be telling you to "circle the wagons" and prepare for potential difficulties.

Reversed Meaning: Repetition

WHEN IT APPEARS REVERSED IN A READING, The Circle suggests that you are drawing the same circle over and over again on your tracing board, rather than doing anything more creative. If the circle is large enough, you may be able to convince yourself that you're going someplace different, because the scenery and the angles keep changing; still, if you pay attention to the distance between you and your goals, you may be in for a surprise.

IN PRACTICAL DIVINATION, this card reversed often means that you are going around in circles, accomplishing nothing beyond what you've already done before. This can be a necessary thing, but it's easy to overdo it. Pay attention to the patterns in your life that seem to repeat themselves over and over again. Are there situations at work, in your relations with other people, or within yourself that show up with clockwork regularity? If so, what might you be doing to foster these patterns? It's common (and convenient) to blame the universe for such things, but most of the time the ruts we get stuck in are the ones we make ourselves.

Exercise for Card 4

For this exercise, you'll need your pen and compass, and several sheets of unlined paper. As in the exercise for Card 3, mark one point on the paper, then another; the two should be close enough together that the two points of your compass can reach easily from one to the other.

Decide which of the two points will be the center of your circle, and put the metal point of the compass exactly onto it, pressing the point into the paper. Widen or narrow the compass until the pencil point comes exactly to the other point, and then twist the handle around to draw a circle, starting and ending at the other point.

If you haven't used a geometer's compass before, it may take you a certain amount of practice before you can do so with any degree of grace. Take the time you need; you'll be drawing a lot of circles in the exercises to come.

A couple of technical terms will help make things clearer in later exercises; if you managed to miss geometry in school, or have forgotten whatever you learned then, you may want to make mental notes. The curved line that you draw with the pencil point of the compass, marking the outer edge of the circle, is called the *circumference*. A straight line that goes through the center of the circle, dividing the circle in half, is called a *diameter*. Half a diameter—that is, a line going from the center to the circumference in one direction—is called a *radius*. An *arc*, finally, is simply part of a circle: a curved line, drawn with a compass, that doesn't go all the way around to connect up with itself.

Meditation for Card 4

Here the process of meditation is the same as before, and the topic is the circle. Start, as before, by imagining a single point in the midst of infinite space. When this image is built up solidly, imagine another point some distance away from the first; hold both of the points in your mind's eye, being aware of the relationship between them, as you did in the meditation for Card 3.

This time, however, let the first point be the center, and imagine the second one beginning to move slowly around it in a circle, like a planet orbiting a star. The two points stay exactly the same distance from each other, and the first point does not move at all. Where the second point passes, it leaves a track that you can see, so that as it finishes its first circuit it has traced a circle in space.

As before, begin to think about what this image might mean to you. Think of circles as they appear in folklore and figures of speech, in nature and in human nature. Consider the subject in a general way for a time, then choose one of the possible trains of thought and follow it to its end, returning to the image and then to the train of thought if your mind drifts away from it.

THE SPIRAL

UNFOLDING • DIMINISHING

5: The Spiral

One of the most ancient patterns in sacred geometry is the spiral. In the ancient chambered tomb at Newgrange in Ireland, which was designed so that a single ray of light shone the full length of the underground passage on one day of the year, spirals carved in the stone serve as markers for the sunlight's position and express teachings now forgotten. Found all through nature as well—in the shells of sea animals, the heads of sunflowers, and many other places—the spiral serves as a powerful image of the unfolding of what is hidden.

Spirals of various sorts can be constructed using the standard set of geometrical tools—the pen, straightedge, and compass—but another method was used in more ancient times, when the toolkit of the sacred geometer consisted of a length of rope and several wooden stakes, and the working surface was the living earth itself. A stake or staff would be driven into the earth, and a rope wound around it; another stake would be tied to the free end, and used to inscribe a spiral in the earth as its holder moved around and around the central stake in ever-widening arcs. A variant of this process will be put to use below in the exercise for this card.

Upright Meaning: Unfolding

When it appears upright in a reading, The Spiral suggests that the design you have begun to draw upon your tracing board has much to unfold, if you allow it to follow the directions and dynamics it has already set in motion. Just as the oak unfolds from an acorn, the smallest portion of a spiral's arc already contains the full outward sweep of the finished spiral in potential; follow that potential, and your design will unfold as it should.

In practical divination, this card upright often means that you are in the early stages of a process, one that may lead much further than you expect. It is usually a favorable sign, unless you're asking whether something can be quickly brought to an end! The Spiral upright counsels patience, attentiveness, and a sensitivity to context, so that the spiral patterns of the future can unfold in their own way.

Reversed Meaning: Diminishing

When it appears reversed in a reading, The Spiral suggests that the design you are drawing is spiralling inwards, tracing ever-smaller arcs around the point where it will finally come to rest. The same inner dynamics that once sent it spinning outward in expanding curves now bring it back again, and attempting to force it around into a circle will only break the continuity of the pattern and leave something artificial in place of the natural dance of spiralling force.

IN PRACTICAL DIVINATION, this card reversed means that the situation or some important part of it is winding down and approaching an end. If you've committed yourself too strongly to the idea that it can circle around endlessly, you may be left turning about in empty space when the natural cycle has completed its course. Expansion and contraction, development and decay, beginnings and endings are all part of the order of things, and it's useful to remind yourself of this when you find yourself thinking that anything lasts forever.

Exercise for Card 5

For this exercise, you'll need some items that aren't normally part of the modern geometer's toolkit. A pushpin (the sort with a cylindrical plastic head), a piece of string approximately four inches long, and some tape will be needed, along with a pencil and a sheet of unlined paper. You also need to find a table or working surface in which you can stick a pin solidly without causing damage you or anyone else will regret later. (If you don't want to mar your desk or table, try putting a piece of tagboard or heavy poster board underneath the paper.)

Start by sticking the pushpin into the center of the paper, and through it, so that it's firmly seated in the working surface beneath. Tape one end of the string securely to the side of the pushpin's head, and the other end to the pencil—the closer to the point, the better. Then, without making a mark on the paper, wrap the string around the pushpin until the pencil is held tight against it (see Diagram E-5).

Now put the pencil point against the paper, and unwind the string by moving the pencil around and around the pushpin. Do it slowly, paying attention to the spiral as it forms. When the string is entirely unwound, stop for a few moments, considering the spiral, and then keep going in the same direction, winding the string back around the pushpin, and producing another spiral that cuts across the first. Finish when the pencil is again held snugly up against the pushpin.

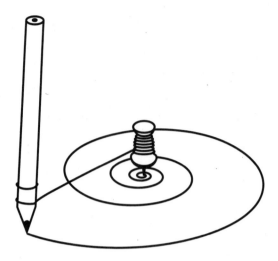

Diagram E-5: constructing a spiral

Meditation for Card 5

Start with the opening process that was described earlier. When you have reached the state of inner clarity, imagine a point in the middle of endless space. See it turning around itself, slowly, in the midst of immensity. Then imagine an arc spiralling out from it, growing wider with each turn, reaching out to a great distance. Finally, as in the exercise, imagine the same arc turning and spiralling back inwards, cutting across the first spiral as it spins back to the center.

When this pattern of imagery is built up solidly in your mind's eye, turn your attention to the next phase of this meditation, and allow images and ideas suggested by the ellipse to take shape in your mind. Be sure to think about both the expanding and the contracting spirals, for each has its lessons.

Consider the spiralling patterns in a general way for a time, then take one train of thought and follow it out to its end. Finish the meditation in the usual way.

6: The Ellipse

A more complex figure, related to the circle but with properties of its own, is the ellipse. An ellipse can be thought of, in some ways, as a circle with two centers. Where a circle is defined by all the points located around a single point (the center) at some particular distance (the radius), an ellipse is defined by all the points located around two points (the foci of the ellipse) in such a way that the total distance from either focus to any of the points and back to the other focus is always the same.

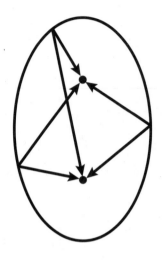

Diagram A-6: the sum of the distances from any point
to the two foci is always the same

All this may seem unnecessarily complicated, but ellipses are all around us. Planets and moons move in elliptical paths as they dance through space, and any object thrown or shot through the air (or through outer space) will follow a curve that's a portion of an ellipse. The ellipse, in fact, is the natural curve of movement and of dynamic energy in the universe of our experience, and it has subtle and important lessons to teach.

Upright Meaning: Flow

WHEN IT APPEARS UPRIGHT IN A READING, The Ellipse suggests that the pattern that is taking shape on your tracing board is defined, like the ellipse itself, by the graceful curves of energy in motion. To the extent that your designs move in harmony with those curves, the flow of energy itself will bring lines and forms to the places they need to be.

IN PRACTICAL DIVINATION, this card upright means that the situation around you is moving in the right direction, and you simply need to move with it. This is nearly always a positive sign in divination, promising not only success but also smooth sailing on the way there. As long as you pay attention to the flow of events, and try to respond to them (rather than to your own preconceptions about the situation), things are very likely to work out well.

Reversed Meaning: Adjustment

WHEN IT APPEARS REVERSED IN A READING, The Ellipse suggests that the pattern that is taking shape on your tracing board requires you to make adjustments in the lines and forms you've already drawn. However attractive these latter may be, they have the potential to come into conflict with the overall design that's taking shape, or with the parts of it you are drawing right now. Like an ellipse, the design before you has more than one central point, and it's necessary for you to make sure that every important factor is able to fulfill its role and its destiny in the whole.

IN PRACTICAL DIVINATION, this card reversed means that the situation you are facing will require you to make adjustments, in yourself or in other aspects of your life. While large-scale changes aren't needed at this time, plenty of minor changes may be needed in order for you to deal with the situation effectively. Sensitivity to subtle factors is important here, and so is attention to detail.

Exercise for Card 6

This exercise, like the last one, requires a working surface into which you can stick pins without causing damage you or anyone else will regret. You'll need two pushpins this time, and a piece of string perhaps eight inches long, as well as a pencil or pen and a piece of unlined paper.

Start by tying the two ends of the string together with a knot that won't slip—a square knot works well—to form a loop. Next, stick the two pushpins into the paper, a few inches apart, and make sure they're fixed firmly in the working surface. Loop the string around the pushpins, and put the pen or pencil in the loop and pull it out until the

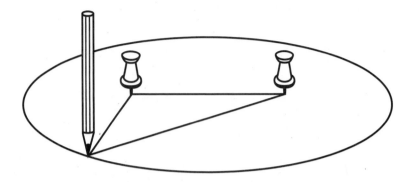

Diagram E-6: constructing an ellipse

string is taut, forming a triangle, before putting the point down against the paper (see Diagram E-6).

At this point, all you need to do is move the pen or pencil to one side, keeping the string loop taut at all times. Let the string slide freely around the pen or pencil and the pushpins. The movement of the pen or pencil and the pull of the string loop will combine to trace a perfect ellipse on the paper, with the two pushpins as its two foci.

Meditation for Card 6

After the same opening process as before, imagine a point amid endless space. After the first point is solidly established in your mind's eye, imagine a second point not far away. Then, as in the exercise, imagine an ellipse taking shape around the two points. Try to sense the way the points around the circumference of the ellipse relate to the two foci, by turns closer to one and farther from the other.

When this imagery is solidly built up, go on to the next phase, and allow this pattern of images to call up ideas and images in your mind. What does the ellipse seem to symbolize? What meanings might it have? As before, consider these things in a general way for a time, then take one train of thought and follow it out to its end. Finish the meditation in the usual way.

THE VESICA PISCIS

UNION • ENCOUNTER

7: The Vesica Piscis

With the vesica piscis, we reach the most important of the basic constructions used in traditional sacred geometry. The vesica is formed out of the overlap between two circles, each one with its center on the other's circumference. A dizzying array of constructions unfold from it; in sacred geometry, few designs rival it as a source of meaningful patterns.

The term *vesica piscis* is Latin, and literally means "vessel of the fish." In Roman times, subtle movements of the Earth's axis were bringing the zodiacal sign Pisces to the point of heaven where the sun stands at the spring equinox, and the followers of a new religion—Christianity—borrowed the vesica from older traditions as a symbol for their beliefs. They left just a little of the two circles at one end, to represent the tail of the Piscean fish. It was a clever use of symbolism; it announced Jesus of Nazareth, whose career was marked with fish miracles and who drew disciples from among fishermen, as the savior of the dawning Piscean Age.

The importance and meaning of the vesica aren't restricted to any one religion, though, or for that matter to any one of the twelve months of the Great Year. Wherever two factors or forces combine to create a more complex unity, the vesica abounds. At every moment, for example, cells in every part of your body are forming and reforming the vesica as they reproduce themselves. In the process of human reproduction and birth, the same thing happens on many different scales. In fact, there's a fully developed sexual symbolism to these basic geometric patterns, with the point as the ovum, the line as the penis, the circle as the vagina, the vesica as the sexual act uniting male and female, and so on. As the ancient masters of sacred geometry taught, everything comes down to geometry in one way or another.

The vesica is especially important because it is the easiest way to generate one of the three primary root relationships of traditional sacred geometry, the $\sqrt{3}$ relationship. About these roots and their meaning, we'll have much more to say as we go on. For now, the important point is that $\sqrt{3}$, the square root of 3, is a very odd number. Mathematicians call it "irrational." It can't be expressed exactly by any fraction or any decimal figure; it "falls between" any measurement in number, no matter how precise. As we'll see, though, it can be expressed exactly in geometrical terms, and it takes on an extraordinary importance in the realm of sacred geometry.

Upright Meaning: Union

WHEN IT APPEARS UPRIGHT IN A READING, The Vesica Piscis suggests that the process set in motion with the drawing of the first point has begin to bear fruit. From the point, the line and the circle have unfolded, the spiral and the ellipse have come into being, and now a second circle has taken shape, producing the vesica, the symbol of creation. The space between the circles is a womb from which any number of things will be born.

IN PRACTICAL DIVINATION, this card upright is usually a sign of success, especially in any question where the actions of others are important. It means that you are not alone, and that other factors, forces, or people are adding their efforts to yours. The situation will improve to the extent that you can work constructively with the others involved. Openness, honesty, and a readiness to give fully of what you have to offer are strongly highlighted.

Reversed Meaning: Encounter

WHEN IT APPEARS REVERSED IN A READING, The Vesica Piscis suggests that the circle you have drawn around yourself no longer contains everything in the picture. A new circle is present, with its center at the very edge of your circle and most of its area outside your reach. Where there was one, there is now two, and this other is not a reflection or a subset, but an equal.

IN PRACTICAL DIVINATION, this card reversed reminds you that the people and patterns of interaction around you have lives and directions of their own, and can't simply be treated as passive tools for your own goals and purposes. When you start a relationship, have a child, launch a career, form a group, take up a spiritual path, or in any other way involve yourself in the lives of others, you make room in your life for patterns and influences that will develop in directions you may not expect or appreciate. When this card appears reversed, it may be telling you that you're not taking the needs and wishes of others into account, or that you may be trying to force someone or something to be what you want, rather than what it is. Either way, there's little good to be gained from such projects.

Exercise for Card 7

For this exercise you'll need your pen and compass, along with a sheet of paper. Start by marking two points on the paper, just as in the exercise for Card 3; choose one as the center, set the points of the compass to equal the distance between them, and draw a circle around the center point, beginning and ending at the other. For convenience, we'll call the two points A and B, with A at the center of the circle you've just drawn.

Then, without changing the distance between the compass points, put the metal point of the compass on point B, where the pencil point started, and the pencil point where the metal point was, on point A. Draw another circle, this time with point B at the center, overlapping the first circle to form a vesica piscis.

The two points where the circles cross are important, so mark them as points C and D. If you were to measure the distance between points A and B, and compare it to the distance between C and D, you would find that if your vesica is drawn correctly—no matter how large or small it happens to be—the relationship between the two distances is always the same: the longer distance (the length of the *major axis*, in geometer's jargon) is always equal to the shorter distance (the length of the *minor axis*) times $\sqrt{3}$, the square root of 3.

Meditation for Card 7

Begin this meditation with the same opening process as before. When you've finished the brief period of focused clarity, start once again by imagining a point in the middle of infinite space. Imagine a second point some distance away from the first, and then, as in the meditation on the circle, picture the second point moving around the first, tracing out a circular track in space.

Let the second point circle the first for a time, and then bring it back to its starting place, where it rests. Next, imagine the first point leaving its place and circling the second, tracing out a track of its own. This track crosses the one already made by the second point, forming the pattern of the vesica piscis.

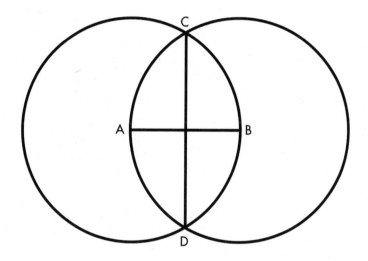

Diagram E-7

Finally, bring the first point back to its starting place, and then imagine both points moving at the same time, each following its own track through space at the same pace. The result is rather like an abstract geometrical dance. (Imagining all this clearly may take a certain amount of practice!)

As with the meditations you've already done, let these patterns of imagery remind you of things in the universe, your life, and yourself that seem similar to them. Draw on anything in the previous discussions that seems useful, interesting, or puzzling. Consider these in a general way, and then choose a particular train of thought and follow it as far as you can. Finish the meditation in the usual way.

THE EQUILATERAL TRIANGLE

FORM • LIMITATION

8: The Equilateral Triangle

One important branch of sacred geometry has to do with what are called *regular figures*—that is, particular geometrical designs in which all the lines are the same length and all the angles are equal to one another. These are important because their very simplicity allows subtle patterns of relationship and meaning to come through clearly.

The simplest of all the regular figures is the equilateral triangle. The word "equilateral" comes from Latin and means "having equal sides," pointing to the most important feature of this particular kind of triangle. Geometers in ancient times divided triangles into three different classes: *equilateral* triangles, which had three sides of equal length to one another; *isosceles* triangles, in which two sides were of the same length but the third was different; and *scalene* triangles, in which each side was a different length from the others. Each of these classes has its own symbolism and special uses.

The triangle is not only the simplest of the regular figures, it's also the most rigid and predictable. If you know the lengths of the three sides of a triangle, you know what the angles have to be; if you know what two of the angles are, you know what the third has to be, and you know the ratios between the lengths of the different sides. In architecture and engineering, too, the rigidity and stability of the triangle have been used since ancient times. If you look at the trusses used to support a bridge or the roof of a house, you'll find that they are composed of a series of triangles for exactly this reason.

Upright Meaning: Form

WHEN IT APPEARS UPRIGHT IN A READING, The Equilateral Triangle suggests that the design you are making has need of the stability and solidity that triangles can provide. Attention to form, to focus, and to a more structured and orderly approach are called to help your hopes and dreams take on ever more real form.

IN PRACTICAL DIVINATION, this card upright means that you may wish to consider bringing some order and structure into the situation you're considering. There are times when vagueness, fluidity, and uncertainty are a source of freedom and spontaneity, but there are times when they lead to confusion and failure instead, and this is one of these latter. This is a time to turn wishes and daydreams into step by step plans so that they can unfold into solid realities.

Reversed Meaning: Limitation

WHEN IT APPEARS REVERSED IN A READING, The Equilateral Triangle suggests that the patterns on your tracing board are subject to limits, whether or not you are aware of this—and whether or not you like it! Keep drawing constantly outwards from the center, and sooner or later you'll run off the edge of the paper; add line upon line, layer upon layer, and eventually you'll reach and pass the point of diminishing returns.

IN PRACTICAL DIVINATION, this card reversed means that you are running up against the limits of the situation, and further efforts aren't necessarily going to get you anywhere. Pounding your head against a brick wall, remember, hurts you much more than it hurts the wall! A little more flexibility and a certain degree of modesty are counseled here.

Exercise for Card 8

Start by drawing a line somewhere not too far from the middle of the paper. On the line, mark two points, which should be labeled A and B. They can be as close or as far apart as you like, but whatever distance you choose will be the length of the sides of your triangle, so plan accordingly. (For example, don't put them so far apart that the third point of the resulting triangle will end up off the paper!)

Put the metal point of the compass on point A, and adjust the pencil point until it rests on point B. Draw an arc up from B until you've made at least a quarter-circle. Now, without changing the setting of the compass points, put the metal point on B, set the pencil point on A, and draw an arc up from A until it crosses the first arc. Mark the point where the arcs cross as point C. (If you've been paying attention, you've probably realized already that this whole process is simply a matter of drawing half a vesica piscis; if you extend the arcs as far below line AB as you did above it, the whole vesica will be formed.)

Then, using the straightedge, draw a line to connect A and C, and another one connecting B and C, to create triangle ABC, just as shown in Diagram E-8.

Meditation for Card 8

Begin with the same process as before. After you've reached the state of inner clarity, imagine the point in infinite space, and then a second point, some distance away from it. Picture a line going from one to the other. While this line, like all lines, can be extended infinitely out through space, for now pay attention only to the segment uniting the two points.

Next, imagine two more lines of exactly the same length, each one connected to one of the two points but not to the other. Imagine them lying together with the first line, and then pivoting upwards, crossing each other. The third line remains in place, unmoving. The two lines continue to pivot until their ends come into contact. Then they stop, forming a triangle.

As before, allow this pattern of imagery to stir reflections and comparisons in your mind, and draw on any material from the foregoing discussions that seems useful. What does the triangle bring to mind in the universe, your life, and yourself? Think about it generally for a time, and then choose a train of thought and follow it to the end. Close the meditation in the usual way.

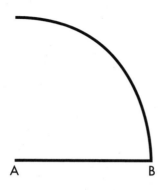

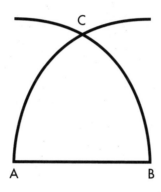

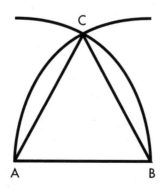

Diagram E-8

9: The Hexagram

Another branch of sacred geometry that has been of great importance down through the years involves *regular polygrams*, star-shaped patterns drawn according to certain specific rules of geometry. The hexagram is one of four regular polygrams that appear in the Sacred Geometry Oracle and, like the others, it's seen a lot of use as a symbol in different spiritual traditions. Most people in the West nowadays know it as the Star of David, the most common symbol of the Jewish faith, but it also has a place in Hinduism, Taoism, and several other traditions that are less well-known.

The hexagram, obviously enough, is formed from two equilateral triangles pointing in opposite directions. Less obviously, it has a special and subtle relationship to the geometries of the circle and the vesica piscis. From these two sets of connections, it draws its principal meanings in the Oracle: from the first, the conflict between opposed forms; from the second, the establishment of harmony in place of conflict.

Upright Meaning: Balance

WHEN IT APPEARS UPRIGHT IN A READING, The Hexagram suggests that the design you're making could well make use of a balance between seemingly opposed patterns. Even though the two triangles of the hexagram seem to be pointing in opposite directions, there's a hidden harmony between them, and by bringing this out you can create something of greater beauty and symmetry.

IN PRACTICAL DIVINATION, this card upright means that it's necessary to find a balance between two different factors or forces in the situation. As much as you may wish to accept one and reject another, both of them have a valid place in your life right now, and deserve an equal share of your time and attention. The Hexagram upright often means that you're assuming that it's necessary to choose between two alternatives when, in fact, it's possible to embrace both at the same time.

Reversed Meaning: Conflict

WHEN IT APPEARS REVERSED IN A READING, The Hexagram suggests that the pattern you are creating has come to a parting of the ways. Like arrows, the two triangles before you point in two different directions, and choosing one means giving up the other.

IN PRACTICAL DIVINATION, this card reversed generally means that you're trying to have your cake and eat it too. Like it or not, you need to make a choice between the alternatives in front of you.

There are times when you can get everything you want in a situation, but this isn't one of them; there are other times when trying to have everything may leave you with nothing at all, and this may well be one of those. Make your choice and make it cleanly, and keep in mind that crying over spilled milk doesn't help you any more than it helps the milk.

Exercise for Card 9

Start the exercise for this card by using your compass to draw a circle of any convenient size, and mark a point, point A, on the circumference of the circle. With the setting of the compass points unchanged, put the metal point of the compass on A, and draw an arc as shown in Diagram E-9, crossing the circle's circumference on both sides. If you're paying attention, you'll notice that the arc goes through the mark left by the compass point at the center of the circle, and this may give you a clue about the deep patterns underlying this construction.

Mark points B and F where the arc crosses the circumference, as shown. Then move the metal point of the compass to B and draw another arc, crossing the circumference at A and a new point, which should be marked as point C. Do the same with the metal point at F, crossing the circumference at A and a new point E.

Now do the same thing twice more, once with the metal point at C and once with it at E. If you've placed your points where they should be—and this is a good test of how carefully you're handling the compass—the arcs from C and E should meet at a new point, D, which is exactly opposite your original point A. (If they don't meet, try to figure out where the mistake is, and either correct the drawing you have or give it another try.)

Finally, using the straightedge, draw lines connecting points A and C, C and E, E and A, B and D, D and F, and F and B, to create your hexagram.

Meditation for Card 9

After the usual process of opening a meditation, imagine a triangle; if you like, you can create it in the same way as in the last card's meditation. Hold it in your mind's eye for a moment, and then imagine another one exactly equal to it, set so precisely onto the first triangle that it looks as though there's only one triangle there.

Then imagine the second triangle pivoting slowly and gradually, like the hand on a clock face, until it and the first triangle form a hexagram. Hold the image in your mind's eye for a short time, and then imagine the two triangles changing color, so that the upward-pointing one is red and the downward-pointing one is blue.

Go on to allow the image to call up images, ideas, and associations as before; think about these generally for a time, and then choose a particular train of thought and follow it out to the end. Finish the meditation in the usual way.

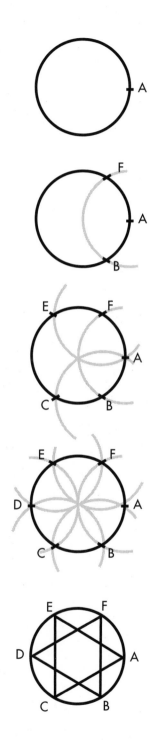

Diagram E-9

10: The Cross

The womb of the vesica piscis bears many things, and one of them is paradox. One of the special gifts that practicing sacred geometry has to offer is a clearer sense of the way that seemingly opposed patterns and processes actually unfold from each other, rely on each other, and return to each other.

In the relation of the vesica to the right-angled cross, this sort of paradox is hard to escape. The vesica is a symbol of creation and birth, while the cross—partly because of its association with the death of

Jesus of Nazareth, but not entirely so—has come to symbolize conflict, suffering, and death. At the same time, as the exercise for this card will demonstrate, the cross develops from and depends on the vesica, suggesting the unity of birth and death, joy and suffering, love and struggle.

At its root, the cross is a symbol of intersection and interaction, the crossing of two lines at right angles to form a framework of creation, cooperation, or conflict. It's in keeping with this symbolism that Christian mystics have seen the cross of the Crucifixion as the point of intersection between heaven and earth, fall and redemption; equally, though, it's in keeping with the same symbolism that ancient Mexican priests and shamans used it as a symbol for the god of crossroads and merchants, and Plato wrote of it in the *Timaeus* as the intersection of the Same and the Other, the two great cosmological powers that hold the universe in being. All these unfold out of this ancient geometrical symbol.

Upright Meaning: Interaction

WHEN IT APPEARS UPRIGHT IN A READING, The Cross suggests that two or more of the lines in the pattern in front of you are moving toward contact. The result may be positive or negative from your perspective; much depends on the angles of the lines involved, and on their relationships with the larger pattern around them. Where the lines cross, a point will be formed, with all the symbolism of beginnings and commitments that implies.

IN PRACTICAL DIVINATION, this card upright usually refers to some form of contact between people, things, or parts of your life that have been separate up until now. It's a sign of meetings, of new personal or professional relationships, of forces combining in a dizzying variety of ways. From these combinations, changes will unfold; one way or another, you won't be quite the same person afterwards. In the future, you'll look back on this situation as a crossroads in your life.

Reversed Meaning: Dissension

WHEN IT APPEARS REVERSED IN A READING, The Cross suggests that two or more of the lines in the drawing before you are crossed inappropriately, bringing confusion and interference into the pattern. To take crossed lines and bring them into parallel takes a good deal of care and patience; rushed or fumbled, the attempt simply moves the point of crossing from one place to another without resolving the underlying situation.

IN PRACTICAL DIVINATION, this card reversed means that the various factors or forces in the situation are in conflict with one another. You may be working at cross-purposes with someone else, you may have gotten your signals crossed, or you may simply find yourself being unusually cross with others—and all these figures of speech communicate a good deal about the challenging potentials of this card. To draw on one more figure of speech, it can be a difficult cross to bear.

Exercise for Card 10

The exercise for this card is based on the vesica piscis, but it moves in new directions, and introduces a method we'll be using in many of the exercises to come. You may wish to pay careful attention to the following steps, and practice the method several times to make sure you've worked out any difficult parts.

Start by drawing a line, and marking points A and B on it. Now make a vesica with line AB as the minor axis: that is, set the compass points to the distance between A and B; with A as the center point, draw an arc up and down from B, through a half-circle; then, with B as center, draw an arc up and down from A, crossing the first arc above and below the line. Mark the points where the two arcs cross as C and D. Using the straightedge, draw in line CD, and where it crosses line AB, mark point E (see Diagram E-10).

The two lines AB and CD now form a right-angled cross, with point E as its center. It's worth mentioning that, if you followed the instructions, E will be exactly halfway between A and B, and also exactly halfway between C and D. Any time you need to divide a line segment in half geometrically, this is one way to do it.

Meditation for Card 10

After the usual opening, imagine a line; if you like, you can start out as before with the point in space and construct the line from it, as in the meditation for Card 3. Choose a point on the line, and then imagine another line crossing your first line at right angles, in the same way that line CD crossed line AB in the exercise from Card 7.

The cross you've formed consists of two lines, but it also emphasizes one particular point—the point of intersection between the two lines. As the commentary above suggested, this has the same symbolic meanings as any point, and this brings up an interesting idea. Two points, as we've seen, define a line . . . but equally, two lines define a point.

This idea is the topic for your meditation. After you've built up the imagery in your mind's eye, recall what you know about points and lines, along with anything useful from the discussion above, and try to grasp what the idea just mentioned implies in the universe, your life, and yourself. Think about it generally for a time, then follow one particular train of thought as far as you can. Finish in the usual way.

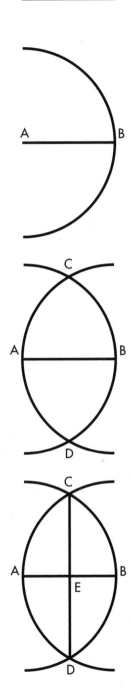

Diagram E-10

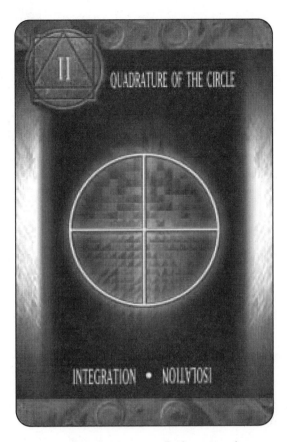

II: Quadrature of the Circle

The phrase "quadrature of the circle" has had two different meanings in geometrical writings over the years, and a certain amount of confusion has come about as a result. On the one hand, it stands for the relatively simple process of dividing a circle into four quarters, producing the symbolic pattern that is the subject of this card. On the other, it represents the supreme challenge and magnum opus of traditional sacred geometry, also called "squaring the circle"—the construction of a square and a circle of exactly the same area or perimeter, the subject of Card 32.

For our purposes, "quadrature of the circle" will keep the first of these meanings, but there's a point to the connection. Simple as it is to construct, the circle divided into four equal parts is a symbol of profound importance in many of the world's spiritual and esoteric traditions. In many Native American cultures, as well as in European pagan traditions and the inner disciplines of Western occultism, the quadrated circle is a symbol of the world itself. Its four quarters echo the four directions, the four seasons, and the four symbolic elements, as well as many other fourfold patterns that shape the universe of our experience. The presence of these patterns makes the quadrated circle also a symbol of wholeness, of integration and completeness.

For each of us, the world is defined and created by the sum total of things within reach of our awareness. Thus in an important sense, it's true to say that each of us lives in a different world, since no two people are aware of exactly the same things. Still, the fact that we don't perceive something doesn't mean that it doesn't exist; each human world has its boundaries, however near or far away they may be, and outside those boundaries lie other worlds we have never imagined.

Upright Meaning: Integration

WHEN IT APPEARS UPRIGHT IN A READING, Quadrature of the Circle suggests that it's time to pull together the design you're drawing into a unified whole. There are lines that have not yet been drawn, arcs and circles that have not yet been traced, patterns and shapes you have not yet linked together into the broader design, and now is the time to pay attention to these things. Seek completion and integration; pay attention to the overall shape of what you are striving to create.

IN PRACTICAL DIVINATION, this card upright means that you may need to focus more on the whole picture, and less on its individual parts. You may be tangled up in details that would be better off left for another time, or delegated to someone else; you may also simply be worrying too much about things that will take care of themselves. Balance, perspective, and a sense of humor are highlighted now.

Reversed Meaning: Isolation

WHEN IT APPEARS REVERSED IN A READING, Quadrature of the Circle suggests that the circle you have drawn around the edges of your design might best be treated as a boundary for the time being. The patterns and relationships within the circle need your attention right now; those outside it can wait a little longer. Once the design within the circle is complete, you'll have a clearer idea of how to link it up with the wider picture.

IN PRACTICAL DIVINATION, this card reversed usually means that your energies need to be turned inward at this time, toward yourself rather than toward the world. This can be a sign that you need to spend more time alone, putting your own life in order. You may have become too deeply caught up in the concerns and activities of those around you, or you may be trying to run away from difficult issues or insecurities by hiding from yourself in a flurry of projects and commitments; either way, you run the risk of becoming the weak point in your own plans. Take the time to deal with your own issues and needs now, even if that means putting the rest of the world on hold for a little while.

Exercise for Card 11

This exercise, like the last one, uses the construction of the cross from the vesica that was introduced in the exercise for Card 7. Begin by marking point A somewhere near the center of the paper, and drawing a circle around it, using the compass. (The circle should be no more than half as wide as the sheet of paper, or you'll run off the edge of the paper later on in this construction.)

Then, with the straightedge, draw a line that goes through point A at the center of the circle and extends out to the circumference on both sides. Where the line cuts across the circle's edges, mark points B and C. Now, using line BC as the starting point, construct a vesica piscis outside the circle: set the compass points to the distance between B and C, and first with B as center, then as C, swing a pair of arcs up and down to intersect above and below the circle, forming the vesica.

Mark points D and E at the two ends of the vesica's major axis, and draw line DE. If you've followed the instructions, it should pass through point A, the center of the circle, and form a right-angled cross with line BC, accomplishing the quadrature of the original circle (see Diagram E-11).

You may want to save the paper from this exercise, as you'll need to do exactly the same construction for the next one.

Meditation for Card 11

After the usual opening process, imagine a circle; if you like, you can do this following the same process you used in the meditation for Card 4. Next, pay attention to the center point of the circle, and then imagine lines extending out of the center point, reaching out to the circle's edge and dividing the circle into four equal parts.

At this point, turn to the topic of the meditation, which is the presence of fourfold patterns in the world we experience. Think of north, south, east, and west; spring, summer, fall, and winter; dawn, noon, sunset, and midnight; birth, life, death, and the after-death state. If you're familiar with the four traditional elements—air, fire, earth, and water—they can be included, and any other fourfold pattern that comes to mind can be added as well. See how these different "quadratures of the circle" echo one another, and seek out the lessons they have to teach about the universe and our place in it.

As before, think about the topic in a general way for a time, then choose a particular train of thought and follow it out to the end. Finish in the usual way.

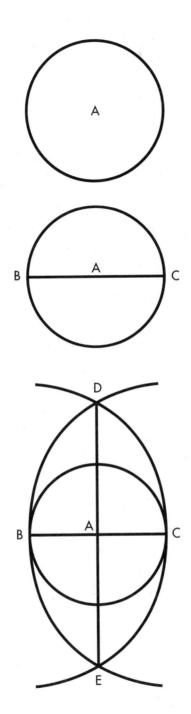

Diagram E-11

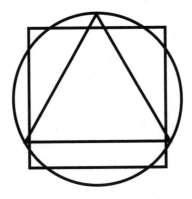

The Second Circle

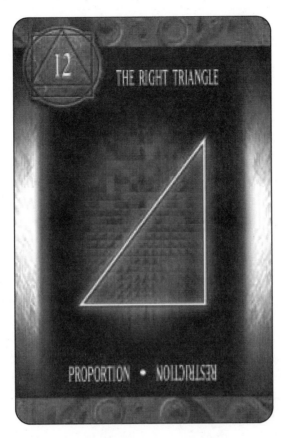

12: The Right Triangle

Along with the equilateral triangle, the subject of Card 8, the traditions of sacred geometry give special attention to another, very specific kind of triangle. This is the sort known as the *right triangle*. Right triangles can be either isosceles or scalene. What unites them with one another, and sets them apart from all other triangles, is that one of their three angles is a right angle—that is, an angle of ninety degrees, one-quarter of the full circle.

Right angles have a whole range of special properties, some simple, others very complex. The important point for our present purposes is that the right triangle represents the first step toward a new factor in the designs and diagrams we've been working with—a factor that will be of increasing importance as we proceed.

A look back through the cards we've already covered may help clarify things. Aside from the fundamentals of point, line, and circle, and the blank space of The Unmarked Card on which they manifest, everything we've done so far has been derived from the vesica piscis and partakes of its special geometrical function, the $\sqrt{3}$ relationship. The right triangle can also be generated out of the womb of the vesica, but it marks the transition from the $\sqrt{3}$ to a different set of functions and processes dominated by $\sqrt{2}$—the square root of 2.

The full $\sqrt{2}$ relationship doesn't appear until Card 20, but the steps by which it unfolds from the vesica and the fundamentals of geometry will occupy several cards before then. Each of these steps adds a concept and a quality of its own, and the right triangle is no exception. What it adds is the idea of proportion, of a relationship between different factors that are not equal—as the two opposed triangles in Card 9 are equal—but make something more than the sum of its parts.

In turn, proportion implies the idea of restriction. Once you've linked things together into a proportional relationship, you can only change them in ways that the relationship permits, and certain other kinds of relationship are no longer possible. To enter into this sort of interconnection is to surrender certain kinds of freedom, and it's always wise to weigh what you'll gain against what you must lose.

Upright Meaning: Proportion

WHEN IT APPEARS UPRIGHT IN A READING, The Right Triangle suggests that the lines in the diagram before you can and should be brought into some sort of proportion, a relationship that will allow each to play its part in a wider unity. This is a card of synthesis, pointing to a time when parts can be brought together to form a new oneness. Everything you see is a piece of the puzzle; what matters now is how you put them together.

IN PRACTICAL DIVINATION, this card upright means that a range of different factors or forces in the situation need to be brought into some sort of relationship with one another. Unlike Card 9, which requires a balancing act between two equal and opposite forces, The Right Triangle upright calls for you to sort out a wider range of factors; at the same time, it doesn't insist on equality. Some factors may play a large role, others will play a much smaller one, and your job is to figure out which is which and decide how much of your time, attention, and other resources each one deserves.

Reversed Meaning: Restriction

WHEN IT APPEARS REVERSED IN A READING, The Right Triangle suggests that all the lines you see before you are already part of a pattern. Even if one line seems small and unimportant, to change it is to change the whole pattern and to affect every individual part of the change as well. The interconnectedness of things can leave you with options that are more limited than you may like.

IN PRACTICAL DIVINATION, this card reversed means that you can't change one part of the situation without everything else changing too. If you are considering a specific change, it may mean that the other factors in the picture will put that change out of your reach, or it may mean that the other factors will be affected by the change in ways you don't expect and may not welcome. In other situations, The Right Triangle reversed often means that relationships between the different factors and forces have settled firmly into place and will put restrictions on what you can do.

Exercise for Card 12

In geometrical terms, a right triangle can be constructed in a number of ways. The exercise that follows does the trick using the vesica and the cross, using the construction we explored in the exercise for the last card.

Start by making a vesica and unfolding a cross from it, just as in the last exercise; if you like, you can simply use the same sheet of paper. Next, choose any two points you like, one somewhere on line BC, the other somewhere on line DE. (To make the process of drawing clearer, neither point should be too close to A, although geometrically speaking any point beside A itself is fair game.) Label these points F and G (see Diagram E-12).

With the straightedge, draw in line FG. No matter where you put F and G, triangle AFG will be a right triangle, because all four of the angles made by the crossing of the lines at E are right angles. You may wish to draw in a number of different points and lines, and consider the resulting triangles.

Meditation for Card 12

Start with the usual opening. Go on from there as in the meditation for Card 10, by imagining a pair of lines intersecting at right angles, each line stretching out to infinity in both directions. Now, as in the exercise, imagine a pair of points, one on one line, one on the other, and picture in your mind's eye a third line connecting these two. Allow the points to move up and down the lines, one at a time or together, and see the line that connects them forming many different relationships with the two intersecting lines. Each of these relationships makes a right triangle; every one of these triangles is different from the others, but every one has an identical right angle as its base and foundation.

After you've built up this image in your mind's eye and explored it, turn your attention to the ideas of freedom and limitation. How much of a right triangle is free to change? How much of it is not? How does this relate to the universe, your life, and yourself? Use any part of the previous discussion that you find useful. As before, think about the topic in a general way for a time, and then follow one particular train of thought out to its end. Finish the meditation in the usual way.

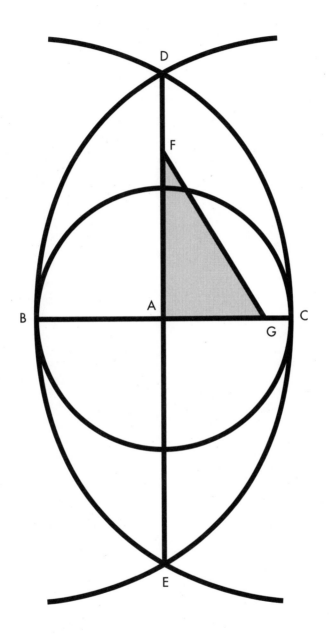

Diagram E-12

THE SQUARE

MANIFESTATION • INERTIA

13: The Square

The square, like the circle and the triangle, is one of the basic geometric shapes we all learn in early childhood. Its role in sacred geometry is equally basic. As we'll see, the square and the circle between them sum up the entire path of sacred geometry in one sense, with the triangle (and, on another and deeper level, the pentagon and pentagram) mediating between them. In another sense, the relation between circle and square is the great problem that sacred geometry—and, indeed, all of life—is meant to solve.

As with some of the other basic figures, a lot can be learned about the square by paying attention to the figures of speech that use it. We may speak of a square meal or a square deal, or describe something as fair and square. A difficult problem may have to be faced squarely. At the same time, if we're too rigid socially, we might end up being called a square.

Symbolically, the square represents the Earth, while the circle stands for the ever-turning heavens. The square is matter, the circle spirit; the square is complete manifestation, the circle complete potential. The square can be known and measured, while the circle is elusive, transcendent. The perimeter of a square—the distance around its outside edge—is always exactly four times its width; the circumference of a circle is equal to its diameter times the irrational number π, pi, which (like $\sqrt{3}$, and several other factors we'll encounter a little later on) can never be expressed exactly as a fraction or a decimal number.

With the square, in other words, we are dealing with the here-and-now realities of the manifested world around us. Relating that world to the realms of spirit and meaning is one of the central tasks of every form of inner practice, and it dominates the higher reaches of the art of sacred geometry.

Upright Meaning: Manifestation

WHEN IT APPEARS UPRIGHT IN A READING, The Square suggests that the designs on your tracing board are ready to take on solidity and reality. The plans are complete, the details have been worked out, and the workers and raw materials are ready and waiting. Remember that once your designs are "off the drawing board," they are at least partly in the hands of other people, who may or may not do exactly what you have in mind.

IN PRACTICAL DIVINATION, this card upright usually means that your plans and hopes are heading toward completion. It can be a symbol of success, like Card 7, but it often represents the end of a series of events, rather than a beginning; what you achieve now will be complete in itself, and may not lead to anything further. Very often, it simply represents the end of a process, the way that Card 1 represents the beginning.

Reversed Meaning: Inertia

WHEN IT APPEARS REVERSED IN A READING, The Square suggests that you've ended up doing the same thing over and over again on the tracing board in front of you. Perhaps you've run out of ideas, or perhaps you've simply gotten caught up in an endless series of straight lines and right angles. Either way, unless you try something different, the pattern you make is likely to turn out pretty monotonous.

IN PRACTICAL DIVINATION, this card reversed usually means that you have stopped exploring new options, and until you overcome your own inertia nothing around you is going to be any different; you're unlikely to see a change in the scenery, in other words, if you're sitting in a parked car. It can also mean simply that the situation is what it is, and nothing much that you can do is going to change that fact.

Exercise for Card 13

There are several different ways to construct a square geometrically, but the one we'll use here unfolds from the patterns we've already used. Start by following the instructions for the exercise for Card 11, exactly as given; if you prefer, you can simply take the design you made in that exercise, and use it for this one. It's possible to make a perfect square simply by connecting the four points where the lines of the right-angled cross intersect the circle, but there's another way to unfold a square from the quadrated circle that's a little more interesting.

First, mark the four points where the cross intersects the circumference of the circle; label them points F, G, H, and I. Then, set the compass points so that they are exactly the same distance apart that they were when you drew the original circle. (This is critically important.) Check your measurement by putting the metal point of the compass on point A, and making sure that the pencil point comes exactly over the circumference of the circle.

Once the compasses are set correctly, put the metal point on point F and swing an arc around through at least half a circle, making a vesica piscis with the original circle and leaving plenty of arc on either end, as shown. Do the same thing with points G, H, and I as centers, producing a flowerlike pattern. The ends of each arc should cross two others; mark points J, K, L, and M at the crossings. Then draw in lines JK, KL, LM, and MJ to create square JKLM, which (again, if you've followed the instructions exactly) should fit precisely around the original circle (see Diagram E-13).

Meditation for Card 13

After the usual opening, start by visualizing a point in the middle of infinite space, as before. Imagine the point moving a certain distance, leaving a visible track behind it, and forming a line. Next, imagine the line moving sideways, at right angles to the first motion, but covering exactly the same distance. The line leaves a track behind it as well, and this forms a square in space.

When you've built up this image solidly in your mind's eye, move on to the topic, which is the square. Any of the material covered in the discussion above is fair game, but try to think of it in terms of the pattern of images just outlined: the point becoming the line, the line becoming a square. Don't hesitate to draw on your meditations on the point and the line to help you make sense of this pattern.

As before, think about the topic generally for a time, and then take one train of thought and follow it as far as you can. When you're done, finish in the usual way.

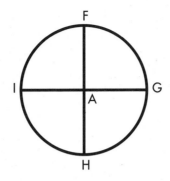

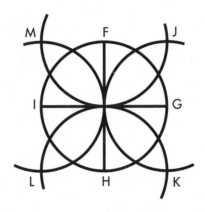

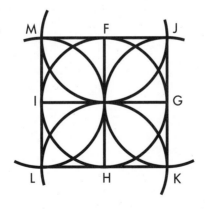

Diagram E-13

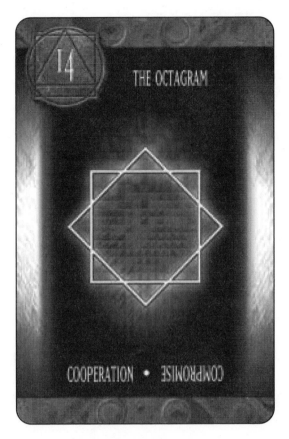

THE OCTAGRAM

COOPERATION • COMPROMISE

14: The Octagram

The octagram, or eight-pointed star, relates to the square in the same way that the hexagram or six-pointed star relates to the equilateral triangle. Like the hexagram, the octagram is an important figure in traditional sacred geometry, and for many of the same reasons. The hexagram is a major factor in the *ad triangulum* system of geometry, one of the two standard approaches to using sacred geometry in practical design. Similarly, the octagram was much used in the rival approach, the *ad quadratim* system of geometry.

In the Islamic world, where eightfold symmetry and symbolism have long been important in mystical teachings, octagons and octagrams appear frequently both in sacred geometry and in its practical applications, such as architecture. Less commonly used in the West, it can still be found in many of the great cathedrals of Europe, and it also plays a central part in the symbolism of certain esoteric spiritual schools.

For our present purposes, the octagram can be seen as a symbol of interactions between two firmly established forces or factors. The form shown here—made by the interlacing of two squares—is best suited to this symbolism. As we'll see in the exercise for this card, there is also a second form of the octagram that links up to somewhat different energies and symbols, and the relation between the two has much to teach.

Upright Meaning: Cooperation

WHEN IT APPEARS UPRIGHT IN A READING, The Octagram suggests that the design you have worked out on the tracing board needs another, perhaps from an outside source, to complete and perfect it. While it's a sign of skill to recognize what you can do, it's a sign of wisdom to recognize what you can't or shouldn't attempt by yourself. Seek the one who can complete what you have begun, and has begun what only you can complete.

IN PRACTICAL DIVINATION, this card upright means that the situation is not something you should try to handle by yourself. Whether it's a friend's advice, an outside perspective, or professional help that you need, you're not going to get it without reaching out to another person and asking for help. This can be a difficult task for many people nowadays, but it's necessary now, and the sooner you accept that fact the less trouble you'll have dealing with the parts of the situation that you *can* handle.

Reversed Meaning: Compromise

WHEN IT APPEARS REVERSED IN A READING, The Octagram suggests that you may not be able to draw the design you had in mind, or develop it in exactly the ways you would prefer. Other factors are present, and whether you like it or not, you are going to have to take them into account. How well you respond to these other factors will have much to do with whether or not your plan has the success you seek.

IN PRACTICAL DIVINATION, this card reversed means simply that you are going to have to compromise. You aren't going to get everything you want out of the situation, and if you keep pushing for the whole pie, you may not even get a slice! This is a good time to rein in your expectations, review the situation (possibly from a less self-centered point of view), and look for the best option that's actually open to you.

Exercise for Card 14

For this exercise, besides plain paper and your geometer's tools, you'll need a pair of colored pencils or pens, of two different colors. Start by drawing a circle of any convenient size with your ordinary pen (or pencil). Draw a line across the circle, passing through its center; mark points A and B where the ends of the line cross the circle's circumference. Next, draw two arcs with A and B as centers and the compass points set to the distance between A and B; the result will be a vesica piscis surrounding your original circle. Line up the straightedge on the two points of the vesica, and draw in a line from one side of the circle to the other, going through the circle's center; mark points C and D where this second line intersects the circle's circumference.

Then, put the metal point of the compass on C, set the compass to the distance between C and A, and draw a circle all the way around. With the compass setting unchanged, move the metal point to A and make a pair of small arcs—just long enough to cut across the second circle in the two places where the compass reaches it, one outside the first circle, the other inside. Then do the same thing with the metal point of the circle on B, drawing two more short arcs and cutting the second circle in two places.

Now line up the straightedge on the places where the two short arcs you made with A at the center cross the second circle. (If you've done this correctly, the center of the first circle will fall exactly on the line.) Using this, draw a line running from one edge of the first circle to the other; mark points E and F where the first circle and the line intersect. Do the same thing with the places that the two short arcs made with B as center cross the second circle—again, the straightedge should just touch the first circle's center—and draw another line across the first circle from edge to edge, marking points G and H where the line crosses the circumference.

If you've done all this successfully—and the division of a circle into eight equal parts is no mean work for a beginner—you may not be happy to find out that all this is just preparation for the actual exercise! Still, the exercise itself is simple once the framework is in place. With one of your colored pencils and the straightedge, draw lines connecting points AC, CB, BD, DA, EG, GF, FH, and HE, as shown in Diagram E-14. This forms the same type of octagram shown on the card.

Then, with the other colored pencil and the straightedge, draw lines connecting points AG, GD, DE, EB, BH, HC, CF, and FA, as shown. This produces a different kind of octagram, which is called a *unicursal octagram* ("unicursal" means "following one route," since you can draw the whole thing without lifting your pen from the paper).

These two forms of the octagram have different traditional meanings, and they also have a different intuitive feel—yet both arise from the same pattern of points equally spaced around a circle. This is a reflection of the subtle flexibilities built into sacred geometry.

Meditation for Card 14

After the usual opening process, imagine a circle divided into eight even segments, as in the exercise. Picture lines reaching out from point to point to form first one form of the octagram, and then the

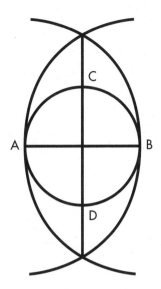

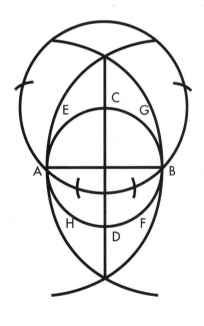
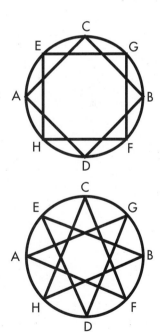

Diagram E-14

other—or, if you're up to this, both of them at the same time! Build this imagery up as solidly as possible in your mind's eye. Then go on to think about the topic for this meditation, which is the relation between your freedom and the freedom of others—between the choices you make in your own life that affect other people, and the choices made by other people that affect you.

As before, consider the topic in a general way for a time, then take one train of thought and follow it out to its end. Finish the meditation in the usual way.

THE DODECAGRAM

COMPLETENESS • COMPLEXITY

15: The Dodecagram

Of the various polygrams, or "stars," that have been used in traditional sacred geometry, the dodecagram or twelve-pointed star is the most
visually complex—although it's actually one of the easier ones to construct. In this figure, the potentials of the ad triangulum geometry
have been taken to the highest level of development that is useful in
practical design. Four equilateral triangles interweave to create this
form of the dodecagram; often associated with the twelve signs of the
zodiac, it serves as a symbol of wholeness and of the full range of possibilities open to us in an infinite universe.

Like the octagram, the subject of Card 14, the dodecagram can actually be drawn in various different ways; this is only one of four possible forms. It can also be made from three interlaced squares, from two interlaced hexagons, or as a unicursal figure—that is, one that can be drawn without raising the point of the pen from the paper. The same pattern of points, in other words, can be connected with triangles, as in the ad triangulum geometry; with squares, as in the rival ad quadratim system; and with other figures as well. This may serve as a reminder that in the whole range of potentials open to us, every factor has a place.

Upright Meaning: Completeness

WHEN IT APPEARS UPRIGHT IN A READING, The Dodecagram suggests that the design before you is approaching completion. This is a good time to pay attention to the lines you haven't finished drawing and the patterns you've only penciled in. If there's anything you planned on including and haven't yet put into your design, it's likely to be now or never.

IN PRACTICAL DIVINATION, this card upright means that the situation is moving toward its final stages. You may need to pay more attention to the details and the fine print, even if this means leaving the bigger picture to take care of itself for a while. At the same time, it's often a sign of approaching success, especially if you have a project under way.

Reversed Meaning: Complexity

WHEN IT APPEARS REVERSED IN A READING, The Dodecagram suggests that the design you are drawing has gotten completely out of hand. Too many lines and forms, too many details and interconnections crowd the tracing board before you. You may have to make the design simpler; on the other hand, you may simply have to erase it and start over again.

IN PRACTICAL DIVINATION, this card reversed usually means that in one way or another, you've gotten in over your head. It may mean that you've tried to accomplish more than the time and resources will permit, that there are more angles to the situation than you had realized, that your plans aren't adequate for the job at hand— or all of these at once! This may be a good time to look at more modest possibilities; alternatively, it may simply be necessary to call it quits and try something else.

Exercise for Card 15

This exercise uses the basic set of geometer's tools and plain, unlined paper. Start by using your compass to draw a circle of any convenient size. Then, with a straightedge, draw a line going through the center of the circle and extending out to the circumference on both sides. Mark points A and B at the two places where the line crosses the circumference.

Next, starting at point A, follow the method you used in the exercise for Card 9 to construct a hexagram; your compass should stay set to the width you used to create the original circle.

Now choose a point where the lines making up the two triangles cross. (Any of the six points of intersection will do equally well; see Diagram E-15.) Line up the straightedge on the point you've chosen, and the center of the circle; you'll find that it goes through another point of intersection on the opposite side of the center. Draw a line through the point and the circle's center, extending it all the way to the circle's circumference on both sides. Mark points C and D where the line crosses the circumference of the circle. Now, just as before, follow the instructions given in the exercise for Card 9, and construct a second hexagram. The two hexagrams join together to create a dodecagram.

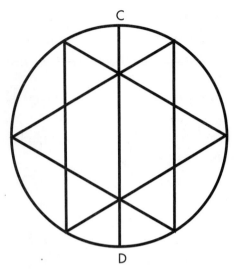

Diagram E-15: one of six possible CD lines

Meditation for Card 15

After the usual opening process, imagine an equilateral triangle. Once it is solidly built up in your mind's eye, imagine another, pointing in the opposite direction, so that you now have a hexagram. Then imagine a third, pointing off at a right angle to the first two, and finally a fourth, pointing the opposite direction of the third.

Think of the way that the four triangles point in four different directions, and imagine a square that surrounds the four points. (If you've worked at developing your visualizing abilities in these meditations, you may even be able to imagine the three squares that make up the second form of the dodecagram, overlaying the triangles that make up the first form.) Once you've explored the way that the triangles join together to define squares, turn to the topic of this meditation, which is the relation between unity and complexity. The dodecagram is a unity composed of other unities—and so is everything else in the universe. What do the individual parts bring to the whole? What does the whole bring to the parts?

As before, consider the topic in a general way for a time, then take one train of thought and follow it out to its end. Finish the meditation in the usual way.

THE TETRAHEDRON

ENERGY • DISRUPTION

16: The Tetrahedron

The patterns we've explored so far all take shape in the two dimensions of the traditional tracing board. The realm of sacred geometry also reaches into the third dimension, however, and makes use of solid shapes of various kinds. Most important among these are five shapes of a very particular kind, which are called the Platonic solids. (They have this name because the ancient Greek philosopher Plato discussed them in detail in one of his most famous dialogues, the *Timaeus*.)

The five Platonic solids are to three-dimensional shapes what regular figures (mentioned in our discussion of Card 8) are to two-dimensional shapes. In a Platonic solid, all angles are identical, all edges are the same length, and all sides are the same shape and size. As with the regular figures, too, the simplicity and consistency of the Platonic solids allow the underlying patterns of the geometric universe to come through with unusual clarity.

The Platonic solids also have an important role in geometric symbolism. Among many other things, they are traditionally related to the five elements of ancient spiritual and magical lore: fire, air, water, earth, and spirit. According to the lore, these elements are the basic patterns of the universe of our experience, present everywhere and in all things.

The tetrahedron, the first and simplest of the Platonic solids, is formed of four equilateral triangles. Among the elements, it is associated with the element of fire. In its broadest sense, the element of fire is equivalent to every kind of energy, and to all things that cause change. It serves as a marker for energy in every part of our experience.

The connection between the tetrahedron and fire is partly a matter of visual form—it looks like a flame, after all—but it also has deeper roots. One part has to do with an interesting point about the Platonic solids. If you mark a point in the center of each side of a Platonic solid, and connect these points together across the inside of the solid with straight lines, you'll get another shape. In four cases, you'll get a different Platonic solid. In the case of the tetrahedron, on the other hand, what you'll get is a smaller tetrahedron (as shown in Diagram E-16). Like fire, which converts all things into itself, the tetrahedron is its own beginning and ending.

Upright Meaning: Energy

WHEN IT APPEARS UPRIGHT IN A READING, The Tetrahedron suggests that the pattern you are drawing has energy as a central feature. The lines on the tracing board are lines of energy, and if you trace them with skill they will lead the currents of power in directions that will take you where you wish to go.

IN PRACTICAL DIVINATION, this card upright means that you are dealing with a great deal of energy in the situation before you— more, perhaps, than you realize. The levels of energy you are dealing with will have to be handled carefully and attentively, so that the energies in the situation don't break loose and cause damage by their sheer force. If you can keep things in hand, though, The Tetrahedron upright is a positive sign, for it usually means that you will have the power you need to bring about the changes you desire.

Reversed Meaning: Disruption

WHEN IT APPEARS REVERSED IN A READING, The Tetrahedron suggests that the design you have created is not solid enough to contain the forces you intend to call into it. The lines on the tracing board may seem firm enough, but they may turn out to be inadequate when the design is put into the hands of the builders and the structure has to face the energies of the real world.

IN PRACTICAL DIVINATION, this card reversed usually means that you've miscalculated the level of energy in the situation; either you don't have access to the energy you would need to bring about what you wish, or there are other forces in the picture that will interfere with what you are trying to do. Disruption, confusion, and chaos are the likely outcomes. When this card appears reversed, you may find that it's necessary to go back to the beginning and start over, or at best to batten down the hatches and prepare to ride out the storm.

Exercise for Card 16

For this exercise, besides the usual tools, you'll need a pair of sharp scissors or a craft knife, and some clear tape; you can also use a heavier type of paper than usual.

Start as in the exercise for Card 11, by drawing a circle, and then another circle of the same size, with its center on the first circle's circumference. Choose one of the two points where the circumferences of the two circles cross, and make a third circle of the same size with its center on that point.

You now have a pattern of three overlapping circles, forming three overlapping vesicas. In the center of the pattern is a space like a rounded triangle, where all three circles (and all three vesicas) overlap. Mark points A, B, and C at the corners of this space. Then mark points D, E, and F at the outward corners of the three vesicas. The result should look like the diagram.

Using the straightedge, draw in lines AB, BC, and CA to form triangle ABC, and draw in lines DE, EF, and FD to form triangle DEF. Triangle ABC is in the center of DEF, and the parts of DEF that are outside ABC form three more triangles, each of them identical to ABC.

Now, with the scissors or knife, cut along lines DE, EF, and FD to separate triangle DEF from the rest of the paper. Carefully fold the paper along AB, BC, and CA, creasing the paper along these lines, so that the three points D, E, and F come together, forming a tetrahedron. Use pieces of tape to join the edges and make your tetrahedron stable.

Once you've made your tetrahedron, examine it from all sides, see how it fits together, and try to make sense of it on an intuitive level. If you like, mark points in the center of the four sides, and try to see how these become the points of another, smaller tetrahedron in the middle of the one you've made.

Meditation for Card 16

After the usual opening process, imagine a large equilateral triangle. As in the exercise, imagine its three corners coming together to form a tetrahedron, and build up the tetrahedron in your mind's eye until the image is solid and stable.

At this point, turn to the topic of the meditation, which is the idea of fire. Start with the simple experience of fire—of flame, heat, and light—and go on to think of energy in general and all things "fiery," thinking about how they relate to you and your life. Draw on any of

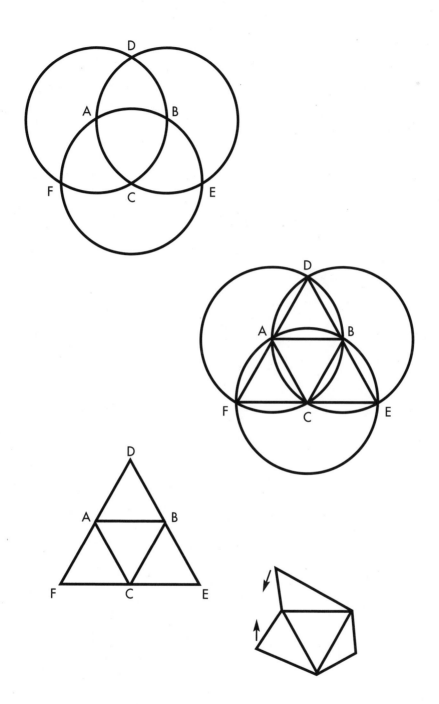

Diagram E-16

the material given above. If you're familiar with any of the traditional teachings about the five elements, go ahead and use this material as well.

As before, consider the topic in a general way for a time, then take one train of thought and follow it out to its end. Finish the meditation in the usual way.

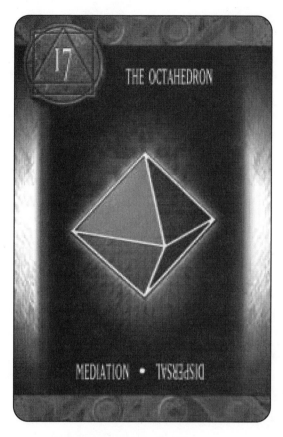

17: The Octahedron

The second of the Platonic solids is the octahedron, which is made of eight equilateral triangles joined together. Like the tetrahedron, it corresponds to one of the five traditional elements—in this case, the element of air.

In the ancient systems of spiritual philosophy that studied the elements, the element of air was especially related to the ideas of mediation, balance between opposites, and flow. Modern scientific ideas bear out these same connections, for it's Earth's atmosphere that mediates between the energies of the sun and the surface of the Earth, balances extremes of heat and cold through the cycles of weather, and flows freely from place to place with its cargo of water vapor—and nowadays, unfortunately, of pollution as well.

The action of the element of air is to unite and balance the other elements. Earth, water, and fire all tend to divide themselves up; there are many different lands, many seas and lakes and rivers, and many different fires—but there is only one sky.

As mentioned in the discussion of Card 16, if you take each of the five Platonic solids, mark points in the exact center of each of their sides, and connect the points across the inside of the solid by straight lines, you'll form a Platonic solid. In the case of the octahedron, the solid you'll create is the cube, the subject of Card 19.

The cube is the Platonic solid assigned to the element of earth. The cube has six sides and eight corners, while the octahedron has eight sides and six corners; both have twelve edges. This suggests a subtle link between the elements of air and earth, one that can also be found in the traditions of ancient spiritual philosophy.

Upright Meaning: Mediation

WHEN IT APPEARS UPRIGHT IN A READING, The Octahedron suggests that the pattern you are drawing has mediation as a central feature. There are a variety of active and passive forms on the tracing board, and your task is to bring them together into a relationship that will benefit all concerned.

IN PRACTICAL DIVINATION, this card upright means that you are in the middle of the situation, with a variety of forces and factors coming to bear on you. While this can be difficult, it allows you to have a major influence on how things turn out, and if you relax and treat the position as a learning experience, the situation may turn out to be a breeze! Gentleness, grace, diplomacy, and the capacity for flow are highlighted here.

Reversed Meaning: Dispersal

WHEN IT APPEARS REVERSED IN A READING, The Octahedron suggests that you are allowing the pattern before you to be pulled about by too many conflicting forces, or scattered into a tangle of smaller patterns with no relationship to one another. Unless you draw it together through your attention and understanding of the whole, the result will be confusion and chaos, not a worthwhile design.

IN PRACTICAL DIVINATION, this card reversed means that you are allowing yourself to become too scattered and unfocused. This may be happening because you are putting too much energy into taking care of other people's concerns, or because you are trying to do too much at once, or simply because you don't know what you want out of the situation and are drifting from one thing to another. Until you decide what you want out of it and take specific, active, and focused steps to get it, you're unlikely to achieve very much, no matter how busy you are.

Exercise for Card 17

As with the exercise for Card 16, this one will call for scissors or a knife, and a roll of tape, along with your usual geometer's tools. Heavy paper may also be worth using.

This construction starts out like the last one, with a pair of circles drawn to form a vesica piscis, and a third circle drawn with its center on one of the two points where the first two circles intersect the lower of the two points. To this you need to add three more circles, as follows. The fourth has its center where the third circle intersects with one of the first two; the fifth, where the fourth intersects with the same one of the first two; and the sixth, where the fourth and the fifth intersect. (Actually, of course, each circle intersects with its neighboring circle at two different places, but if you do the construction as given, you'll find that one of these intersections is always the center of another circle already.) The result is the zigzag pattern of six circles shown in Diagram E-17.

Now draw in the pattern of eight triangles shown in the diagram, using the straightedge. Cut the resulting shape out, cutting only along the outside lines—don't cut between any of the triangles you've drawn! Fold the resulting shape along the lines so that the two lines marked AB are joined together, and fold down the remaining triangles. Use tape to fasten the seams, and you have your octahedron.

As before, take the time to get to know the octahedron, looking at it from different angles and seeking an intuitive sense of the way it fits together. If you like, mark a point in the center of each of its eight sides, and try to see how these become the corners of a small cube in the center of the octahedron.

Meditation for Card 17

Start with the usual opening. When this is completed, imagine an equilateral triangle, as in the meditation for Card 8. Add more triangles, one at a time, until you have formed the same shape you drew and cut out in the exercise. Then, in your mind's eye, fold up the triangles and join edges together to make an octahedron. (If you find it hard to imagine this, make another paper pattern following the instructions in the exercise, and fold it but leave it untaped; then fold it together and let it unfold, concentrating on the process, until you have a clear sense of how it works and can imagine it clearly.)

Once you've built up the image of the octahedron clearly in your mind's eye, turn to the topic of the meditation, which is the element of air. Think about air, about everything connected with air, and everything "airy," drawing on the discussion above and on any knowledge of the traditional lore of the elements you happen to have.

As before, consider the topic in a general way for a time, then take one train of thought and follow it out to its end. Finish the meditation in the usual way.

Diagram E-17

THE ICOSAHEDRON

RECEPTIVENESS • PASSIVITY

18: The Icosahedron

The third of the traditional Platonic solids, and the last of the three made up of triangles, is the icosahedron. This figure is made of twenty triangles joined together. It seems complicated at first glance, but it unfolds from the same patterns that produce the simpler tetrahedron and octahedron.

Of the five traditional elements, the icosahedron relates most closely to the receptive and fluid element of water. In the ancient spiritual philosophies, just as fire is seen as the archetype of all active things, water is the archetype of everything receptive. Where the flames of fire always strive to rise upward, water always seeks to flow downward; where fire creates heat, water brings cold. Between these two opposites, in turn, dances the mediating power of air.

In another application of the ancient symbolism, water is the image of the feminine, while fire represents the masculine. This sort of symbolism can be misunderstood, though, for every human being—whatever his or her physical gender happens to be—contains both fire and water, masculine and feminine sides. Studies of human genetics, echoing this traditional teaching, have shown that the differences between male and female actually involve only about 3 percent of our total DNA.

Like the other Platonic solids, the icosahedron gives rise to another solid if points are marked in the centers of its sides, and these points are connected with straight lines going through the midst of the solid. In this case, the Platonic solid that's created is the dodecahedron, the subject of Card 29. The dodecahedron is associated with the element of spirit, the element that unites and transcends the other four. In earlier times, this subtle link between water and spirit was connected to the opening lines of the Book of Genesis, in which the Spirit of God moved over the face of the waters of creation.

Upright Meaning: Receptiveness

WHEN IT APPEARS UPRIGHT IN A READING, The Icosahedron suggests that the pattern you have drawn has receptiveness as a major factor. The lines and forms on the tracing board before you have drawn energies in from outside sources, and those energies—not the ones you can bring into the design—are best suited to carry your plan to a successful conclusion.

IN PRACTICAL DIVINATION, this card upright means that your best approach in the situation is to take a receptive role rather than an active one. It's a good time to go with the current, in other words, not to try to swim against the tide! However active a role you may have imagined for yourself, there are other people, or different factors, that can take care of the situation better than you can, and if you try to get actively involved you are more likely to create confusion than you are to help. Relax, and let things take their own course; let yourself trust in the wisdom of the universe, rather than trying to rely on your own efforts.

Reversed Meaning: Passivity

WHEN IT APPEARS REVERSED IN A READING, The Icosahedron means that the pattern on the tracing board before you is incomplete, because you have stopped drawing! No outside force is going to take the pen, straightedge, and compass from your hands and create the design you have in mind. Until you pick up the tools and get back to work, you will stay exactly where you are, gazing at a mostly blank board where any number of beautiful and useful things might be taking shape.

IN PRACTICAL DIVINATION, this card reversed simply means that you are waiting for someone or something else to take care of the situation, and that's not going to happen. Until you get up and do something constructive, nothing will change. It's worth remembering, too, a useful slogan from the recovery movement: if you always do what you've always done, you'll always get what you've always gotten.

Exercise for Card 18

Like the last two constructions, this one requires tape and scissors or a knife, along with your geometer's tools, and may benefit from heavy paper as well. This exercise is one of the trickier constructions in this book; you'll want to be as careful as possible when drawing the lines and circles, so that the result comes out. Using the landscape, or horizontal, side of your paper will work best.

Start exactly as in the last exercise, by drawing two overlapping circles, then a third centered on one of their intersections, then a fourth, fifth, and sixth, forming a zigzag pattern of circles, all of them overlapping and forming a double line of vesicas. This time, though, keep on going. You need no less than twelve circles, arranged as in Diagram E-18, to construct an icosahedron. When you've drawn them all out, use the points of intersection to lay out the pattern shown in the diagram.

As before, cut out the pattern, cutting only the outside edge— again, don't cut between any of the triangles, or the result will be a mess! Fold the resulting shape so that all the points marked A come together, and all the points marked B are joined. Fasten the edges with tape, and you have your icosahedron. Take the time to explore it, and if you like, mark a point in the center of each of the twenty sides, and try your hand at imagining how these points become the corners of a small dodecahedron in the middle of the icosahedron.

Meditation for Card 18

After the usual opening, imagine a triangle, and add others one at a time until you have twenty of them, linked together as in the pattern you used in the exercise above. In your mind's eye, fold the pattern up and join the edges until you have a perfect icosahedron.

When this is clear and solid in your imagination, turn your attention to the topic of the meditation, which is the element of water. Think about water itself, the different kinds of fluid that share water's nature and habits, and all the other things in the universe of your experience that seem "watery" in one way or another. Feel free to relate these to any of the points mentioned above, or to anything you may know about the traditional lore of the elements.

As before, consider the topic in a general way for a time, then take one train of thought and follow it out to its end. Finish the meditation in the usual way.

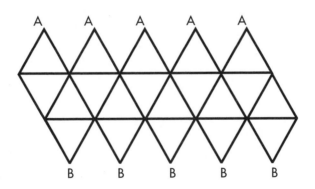

Diagram E-18

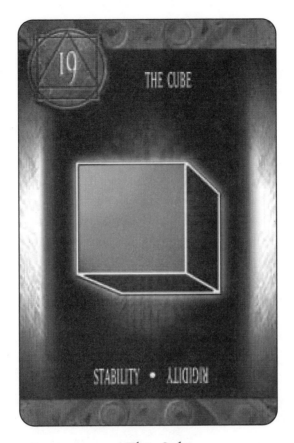

THE CUBE

STABILITY • RIGIDITY

19: The Cube

The cube is the fourth of the five Platonic solids. It's also far and away the most familiar of them; many people don't know what a dodecahedron is, for example, but cubes are another matter. From the blocks we play with as children to the office buildings in which many of us work, the cube surrounds us everywhere.

Stable and solid, the cube is a traditional emblem of the element of earth, one of the five elements of ancient spiritual and magical lore. Of these elements, earth is the densest and most unyielding; it corresponds to what modern scientists call the solid state of matter, just as water corresponds to liquids, air to gases, and fire to energy. The ancient teachings also suggest that the elements form a spectrum, with earth at one end, spirit at the other, and the other elements falling into places in between. In this pattern the cube plays the role of a solid base, from which the other elements rise up and on which they can build.

For all its apparent solidity, though, the cube contains a hidden factor of flexibility. As mentioned earlier on, if you mark a point in the exact center of each side of any Platonic solid, and connect the points together with straight lines inside the solid, another Platonic solid takes shape. In the case of the cube, the result is an octahedron, which symbolizes the mediating and subtle element of air.

The cube also has another remarkable feature. Its faces, of course, are squares, and so if the sides are equal to one, a diagonal line running from corner to corner along one face has a length of $\sqrt{2}$. On the other hand, if you draw a diagonal line between opposite corners of the cube—going not along one face, but through the middle of the cube—the length of that line is equal to $\sqrt{3}$. In the cube, in other words, the two great opposing factors of sacred geometry reveal a hidden unity. This unity will be developed further in some of the cards to come.

Upright Meaning: Stability

WHEN IT APPEARS UPRIGHT IN A READING, The Cube suggests that the pattern on your tracing board is one in which stability plays, or needs to play, an important role. A building needs a secure foundation, and right now so do you and those around you. Proceed with your design, but draw with a steady hand.

IN PRACTICAL DIVINATION, this card upright means that stability is an important factor in the current situation, and one you should not ignore. Too many changes, carried out too quickly, may turn a promising development into a complete mess; if you're growing a garden, it's not a good idea to pull up all the plants once a week to check on how the roots are developing! As the old saying has it, "If it ain't broke, don't fix it"; patience, consistency, and a willingness to let things take shape in their own time are all called for here.

Reversed Meaning: Rigidity

WHEN IT APPEARS REVERSED IN A READING, The Cube suggests that the pattern you are drawing has become so solidly established that it no longer allows for change and growth. Perhaps you have been drawing the same square over and over; perhaps you have been relying too much on straight lines and right angles, and have forgotten about curves and complex shapes. Rigid as it is, the design in front of you may require a lot of erasing and redrawing before it takes on any more flexibility.

IN PRACTICAL DIVINATION, this card reversed means that you've locked yourself into a rigid approach to the situation. Such an approach might work in some cases, but this isn't one of them. You need to lighten up, loosen up, and try something different for a change, even if it seems out of character. Attention to fluidity and flow, to the free dance of energies around the too-rigid walls of the mental prison you've made for yourself, may be useful approaches.

Exercise for Card 19

As with the exercises for Cards 16, 17, and 18, this one works a little better with stiff paper, and a sharp craft knife or a pair of scissors is also needed, along with your geometer's tools. Start by drawing a square of any convenient size, keeping in mind that five more squares of the same size will need to fit on the paper, using the construction from the exercise for Card 13 on pages 79–81.

Next, line up your straightedge with each of the four sides of the square, one at a time, and extend the lines out in both directions (see Diagram E-19). Then set the compass points to the length of one side of the square, and with the metal point set at each of the four corners in turn, draw short arcs to mark off the same distance out from each corner along the lines you've drawn. Connect the marks together, as shown, to make four more squares around the first.

This gives you five of the sides of your cube. To make the sixth, you simply need to repeat the same process one more time, putting the metal point of the compass on the two outer corners of one of the four new squares and making two new marks farther out along two of the lines extending from the original square. Connect these marks to each other to form the sixth square.

Then cut around the outside edge of the pattern—again, don't cut between the squares. Fold and tape the resulting pattern to create your cube. Turn it around and about, looking at it from different sides and seeing the different patterns created by its sides and edges; if you like, mark points in the center of its sides, and try to imagine the octagram formed by linking these points inside the cube.

Meditation for Card 19

After the usual opening process, imagine a square. When this is solidly built up, add another to one side of it. Continue until you have the same pattern you made in the exercise, and then imagine it folding up to create a cube.

Then turn to the topic of the meditation, which is the element of earth. Start with the basic, sensory experience of earth—of soil, sand, gravel, rock—and go on from there to think of all things "earthy," exploring how they relate to you and your life. Make use of any of the material discussed above, and if you've been exposed to the traditional teachings about the five elements, use this as well.

As before, consider the topic in a general way for a time, then take one train of thought and follow it out to its end. Finish the meditation in the usual way.

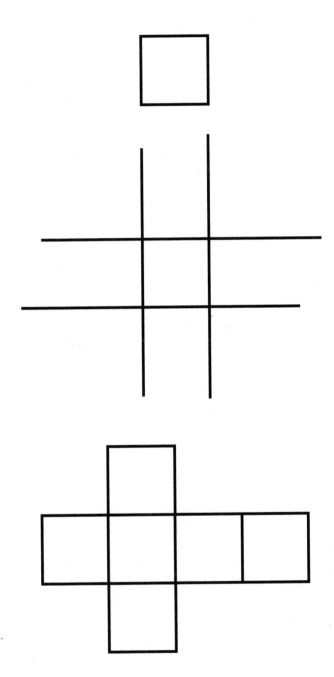

Diagram E-19

20: Square and Diagonal

One of the earliest written accounts of the practice of sacred geometry comes to us from the Greek philosopher Plato, who uses it as a scene in his dialogue *Meno*. There, Plato's teacher Socrates is trying to prove that our minds are not simply blank slates; instead, he suggests that every human being comes into life carrying echoes of spiritual wisdom, and we simply have to learn to remember these.

His method of demonstrating this is interesting. He calls over a servant boy, who has no knowledge of geometry, and leads him step by step through the geometrical process of drawing a square with exactly twice the area of another square. All Socrates does is ask questions; by the end of the scene, the servant boy has not only solved the problem, using the construction we're about to study, but understood it as well.

The relation between the square and its diagonal is a central factor in traditional sacred geometry, and some teachers (modern as well as ancient) put it at the very beginning of instruction. The card shows a smaller square, made of two right triangles, and a larger one, turned at an angle to the first, made up of four of the same triangles. It's clear at a glance that the larger one covers twice the area of the smaller—four triangles rather than two.

What's less apparent at first glance is the special relationship between the length of the sides of the first square and the length of those of the second—or, in other words, the length of the side and that of the diagonal line dividing the smaller square. These are connected by one of the primary root functions of sacred geometry, the $\sqrt{2}$ relationship.

Like the $\sqrt{3}$ relationship, which was introduced along with the vesica piscis in Card 7, the $\sqrt{2}$—the square root of 2—can't be expressed exactly by any fraction or decimal number; no matter how far you pursue it, it "falls through the cracks" of number. Geometrically, though, it's expressed exactly anytime someone makes a square and then draws a line through two opposite corners.

The $\sqrt{2}$ and $\sqrt{3}$ relate to each other in interesting ways. Both represent processes of creation, but they do so from opposite perspectives. Where the $\sqrt{3}$ is formed from the union of two circles, the $\sqrt{2}$ is born from the division of a single square. In the traditional symbolism of sacred geometry, the $\sqrt{2}$ is the image of generation—a label that includes, among other things, human sexuality and birth—while the $\sqrt{3}$ represents relation, the process of interaction by which individuals give rise to more complex unities. In turn, the $\sqrt{5}$, the subject of Card 23 and the key to the mysteries of the Golden Proportion or Golden Section, corresponds to regeneration, the transformative process by which the individual passes beyond old limits and breaks new ground. These three factors are the three primary roots of sacred geometry.

Upright Meaning: Generation

WHEN IT APPEARS UPRIGHT IN A READING, Square and Diagonal suggests that in the design you've drawn on the tracing board are important, untapped possibilities for growth and development. The relationships and patterns before you contain, in themselves, everything you need to take things further, although you may have to look at them in new ways in order to unfold their potentials.

IN PRACTICAL DIVINATION, this card upright is a strong sign of success. It suggests that your efforts in the situation are about to bear fruit, if they have not started to do so already, and that these first results will be followed by others. It often suggests that you are doing the right thing, and should continue with your present plans and activities.

Reversed Meaning: Consequences

WHEN IT APPEARS REVERSED IN A READING, Square and Diagonal suggests that the patterns you've drawn so far may limit what you can do in the future. Before you extend the design any further, you may want to take a hard look at the patterns that have already been set down, and make sure that you are comfortable with the way things will unfold if you go further down the path you've already started.

IN PRACTICAL DIVINATION, this card reversed means that the things you've done and the positions you've taken will have consequences that can't be avoided or ignored. It serves as a reminder that events unfold from what we actually do and say, not from our intentions or our motives. It often means that a course of action you are considering will lead to results that you may not like; in some cases, it can mean that a chain of events has already been set in motion, and the consequences are already coming toward you.

Exercise for Card 20

For this exercise, the usual set of geometer's tools and a plain sheet or two of blank paper are all that's needed. Start by constructing a square, as follows. Draw a line of any convenient length, and mark the two ends of the line as points A and B. Then, somewhere off the line (but not too far away!) and closer to B than A, mark point C. With the metal point of your compass on C and the width set to the distance between C and B, draw a circle; its circumference should cross line AB somewhere along its length. Mark point D where the line and the circle cross (see Diagram E-20).

With the straightedge, draw a new line from D through C, and extend it further until it crosses the circle again above B. Mark point E where the new line intersects the circle. Using the straightedge again, draw a line from B through E. If you've followed the instructions, the angle at B is a right angle.

From this point, making the square is simple. Put the metal point of the compass on point B, set the width to the distance between A and B, and swing an arc up one-quarter of a circle until it crosses line BE. Mark point F at the intersection. Leaving the compass at the same setting, put the metal point on F and draw an arc up from B at least a quarter circle, then move the metal point to A and do the same thing, so that the two arcs cross to form the fourth corner of the square. Mark this as point G. Draw in lines FG and AG to complete the square ABFG.

Draw in line AF, the diagonal of the square. Then put the center point of the compass on G, and with the compass still set to the distance from A to B, draw a circle. (The circumference should pass through A and F.) Using the straightedge, extend line AG to the far edge of the new circle; where the line meets the circumference, mark point H. Then do the same thing with line FG; where the extended line meets the circumference of the new circle, mark point I. Draw in lines AI, IH, and HF to create square AIHF.

If you like, you can then go on to use line IF—the diagonal of the second, larger square—as the side of a new square, which will be four

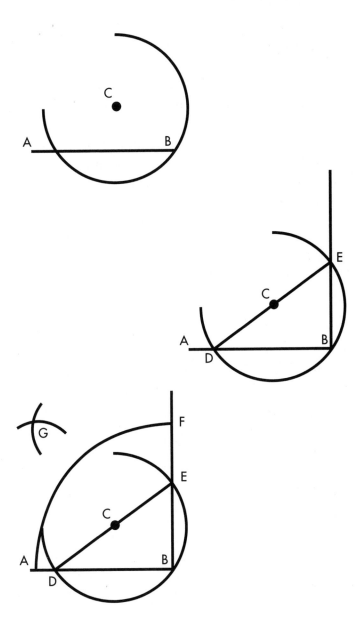

Diagram E-20 (continued on page 123)

times larger than the first one. This process can be continued indefinitely . . . or until you run out of paper to draw squares on.

Meditation for Card 20

After the usual opening, imagine a square; if you wish, you can use the same process as in the meditation for Card 13, extending a point into a line and the line into a square. Once the square is built up solidly in your mind's eye, imagine the diagonal being drawn in. From this, unfold the second, larger square, as in the exercise above.

When you have built this up solidly in your mind's eye, turn to the topic for the meditation, which is creation by division. Explore this idea in the light of any of the comments above that seem useful. As before, consider the topic in a general way for a time, then take one train of thought and follow it out to its end. Finish the meditation in the usual way.

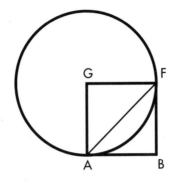

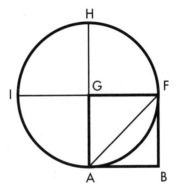

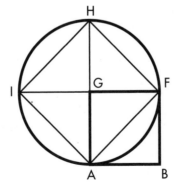

Diagram E-20, continued

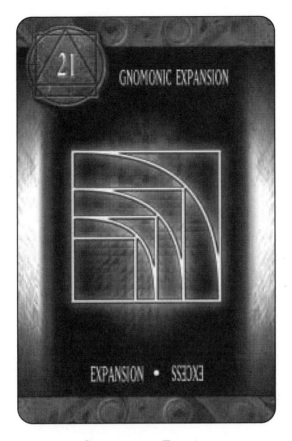

EXPANSION • EXCESS

21: Gnomonic Expansion

Gnomonic expansion is a tool much used by the ancient sacred geometers—a method of producing ever-larger versions of the same form, each version displaying the same proportions as the original. A gnomon was defined in ancient times as "a figure which, when added to an original figure, leaves the resulting figure similar to the original." In less formal terms, the easiest way to think about a gnomon is to imagine two shapes that are exactly the same, except that one is bigger than the other. Put the smaller one on top of the larger, and position it so that no part of the smaller goes past the edge of the larger. The part of the larger shape that remains visible around the smaller one is a gnomon (see Diagram A-21).

Obviously, there are many different possible gnomons for any given shape, but some are more convenient to use than others. Methods for creating the more convenient gnomons for basic shapes were taught to students of sacred geometry in ancient times. In the exercise for this card, we'll explore one of these.

One of the important symbolic teachings connected with gnomons is the equivalence of the very big and the very small. By the process of gnomonic expansion, it's possible to go from a tiny pattern to a huge one, through many intermediate steps, without changing the shape of the pattern itself at all. A minute square and a massive one are both squares, in the same way that an atom and a solar system echo the same structure and follow the same pattern of physical laws.

Upright Meaning: Expansion

WHEN IT APPEARS UPRIGHT IN A READING, Gnomonic Expansion suggests that the design you have traced can be seen as a model for bigger things. What you have drawn on one part of your tracing board may be applicable to a much larger area, if you make sure to do the same thing on the large scale as you did on a smaller one.

IN PRACTICAL DIVINATION, this card upright often means that you may need to pay attention to issues of scale, and to explore the possibility of doing things on a larger scale than you've previously considered. It can be a very favorable sign, suggesting that you are ready for the "big time" and can go on to bigger and better things; it can also mean, though, that you're treating some part of the situation as small and self-contained when it's really the key to the entire picture. In any event, upright Gnomonic Expansion directs your attention to the big picture.

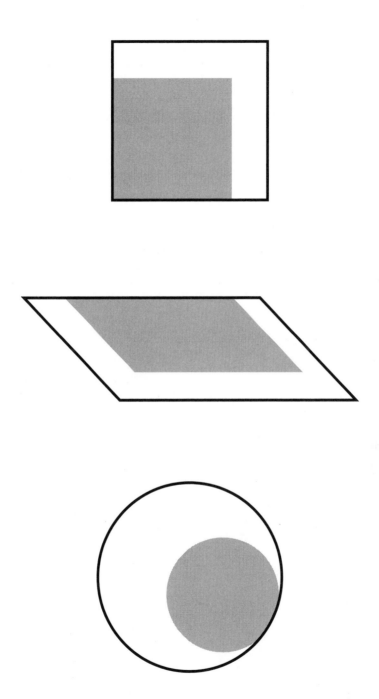

Diagram A-21: the white area in each of these diagrams is a gnomon—added
to the smaller, gray figure, it creates a larger figure of the same shape

Reversed Meaning: Excess

WHEN IT APPEARS REVERSED IN A READING, Gnomonic Expansion suggests that the diagram you've drawn is so large that it's about to spill over the edge of the tracing board! It's a reminder that bigger is not always better, and that a pattern that works well on a small scale can turn into an unwieldy dinosaur when it's expanded beyond its limits.

IN PRACTICAL DIVINATION, this card reversed means that you've gone overboard, and need to back off a little—or a lot. Like Card 20 reversed, Gnomonic Expansion reversed suggests that you've overcommitted yourself, but in a different way; here, it's more likely that you've taken a good thing too far, or allowed past results to convince you that doing the same thing over and over again will always get you what you want. This rarely works for long. As the Taoist master Lao Tsu pointed out, "Too much success is not an advantage; do not tinkle like jade, or clatter like stone chimes."

Exercise for Card 21

For this exercise, you may find graph paper helpful; the ordinary geometer's tools will also be needed.

There are many different ways to create a gnomon for any given shape, and each shape has its own rules. In this exercise, we'll concentrate on one way for creating gnomons for squares, partly because the method is a classic one, partly because you can check your work easily with graph paper.

Start by drawing a square of any convenient size; for the sake of the exercise, it's best if this first square has a whole number of graph-paper squares inside it. Then, with the straightedge, draw three additional lines. All three of these start at the same corner of the square— the lower left corner, let's say (see Diagram E-21). The first goes from there through the upper left corner and on as far as the paper allows, extending one side of the square; the second goes from the lower left

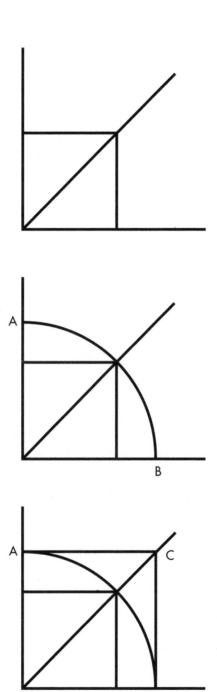

Diagram E-21

corner through the lower right one and on to the end of the page, extending another side of the square; the third goes from the lower left corner through the upper right, forming the diagonal of the square, and going on to the edge of the paper as before.

Now take the compass, put the metal point on the lower left corner, and set the width to the distance to the upper right corner, along the diagonal. Swing an arc to either side of the diagonal until it touches the other two lines. Mark points A and B where the arc and the lines intersect. Then, from A and B, draw lines over and up to the diagonal line. These new lines should be parallel to the sides of the original square. (This can be done by geometrical constructions, but for the time being it's simpler to follow the lines of the graph paper.) The two lines should intersect with the diagonal at the same point; mark this as point C. Points A, C, B, and the lower left corner of the original square form a new square larger than the original. (If you've been paying attention, you've probably noticed that the second square uses a version of the square-and-diagonal construction of Card 20, and so has twice the area of the first square.)

Do this same construction again, taking the square you just drew in place of the original square. Repeat several times, until you've constructed a series of squares, each one larger than the one before it. The L-shaped areas that expand each square to the next are the gnomons constructed by this method.

Again, there are other ways of making gnomons for squares, some of them of very different shapes. You may find it interesting to try to figure out some of the others, and to work out geometrical ways to create them.

Meditation for Card 21

After the usual opening process, imagine a small square. Expand it by way of an L-shaped gnomon, of the sort you constructed in the exercise, into a larger square. Repeat the process again and again, creating ever larger squares. When this pattern of imagery is built up solidly in your mind's eye, turn your attention to the topic of the meditation, which is the relation between the large and the small. Draw on examples from your own knowledge and experience, and use anything that seems useful in the discussions above.

As before, consider the topic in a general way for a time, then take one train of thought and follow it out to its end. Finish the meditation in the usual way.

21: Gnomonic Expansion

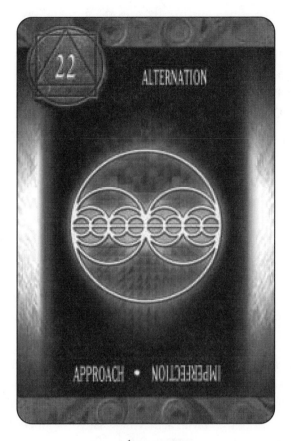

22: Alternation

Another tool much used by the ancient sacred geometers, and well worth exploring by modern students of the art, is a method called *alternation*. Alternation is a way of using ordinary numbers to deal with the "irrational," numerically inexpressible factors that dominate sacred geometry—relationships such as √2, √3, and others we'll explore a little further on. In practical design work, it's important to be able to approximate these factors in whole numbers, and this sort of approximation also forms a bridge between sacred geometry and the science of numbers, another branch of the ancient quadrivium.

You can see alternation at work in an informal way on any modern building site. One carpenter holds up a piece of lumber; another one, with hammer (or nail gun) ready, eyes the join and says, "Up about two inches; down a bit; down a bit more; now up just a hair; okay, hold it right there—" and the nail goes in. Each adjustment is smaller than the one before, bringing the lumber closer and closer to the place it needs to be.

In geometry, the process of alternation is handled by precise constructions, rather than by eye. Still, the principle is much the same, and as we'll see, alternation allows important patterns of meaning to be expressed simply and effectively.

Upright Meaning: Approach

WHEN IT APPEARS UPRIGHT IN A READING, Alternation suggests that the patterns on your tracing board are moving toward their final form, but have not yet achieved it. Lines will need to be moved, forms reshaped, and interactions restructured before you achieve what you wish. Try to save the best of the existing pattern, while bringing the rest up to the same level of quality.

IN PRACTICAL DIVINATION, this card upright means that your goals in the situation are within sight, but not yet within reach. This is a positive sign when it appears in divination, for it means that you're most of the way to achieving what you want, but it also implies that more work will be needed. Patience, persistence, and the ability to learn from your mistakes are all strongly highlighted here.

Reversed Meaning: Imperfection

WHEN IT APPEARS REVERSED IN A READING, Alternation suggests that the patterns on your tracing board will never achieve the perfection you wish. Perhaps you made mistakes in the early phases of the drawing, and it's proceeded too far for them to be corrected now; perhaps your tools, or the materials available to you, simply aren't up to what you had in mind; perhaps you are simply striving for a level of perfection that can't be realized in the world of our experience. For whatever reason, though, your design is flawed, and you will either have to live with that or start over again from the beginning.

IN PRACTICAL DIVINATION, this card reversed means that you are not going to achieve everything you want in the situation, no matter how hard you try. One way or another, there will be imperfections in the end result. It's important to remember that life is always a succession of ups and downs, joys and sorrows, achievements and failures; if you can approach the current situation with this in mind, you may be able to make the best of the situation and enjoy it despite its imperfections.

Exercise for Card 22

To put the principle of alternation into practice, we'll make use of an ancient example. Theon of Smyrna was a philosopher, mathematician, and sacred geometer who lived in the second century of the common era; in his book *Mathematics Useful for Understanding Plato*, he included an example of alternation using the √2 ratio, which we'll follow here. Several pieces of graph paper will be useful.

The goal of this exercise is to create a set of ratios between whole numbers, which will come as close as possible to the √2 relationship. Start by drawing a square on the graph paper with sides equal to one of the paper's squares. Draw in the diagonal. The side equals 1, and the diagonal falls between 1 and 2; you can check this with another piece of the same graph paper. Since we need whole numbers, we set the diagonal number at 1, a little less than the actual length of the diagonal.

Now Theon's method takes over. Add the side to the diagonal, to get the side of a new square; $1 + 1 = 2$, so the second square has sides equal to 2. Now double the side of the original square and add this to the diagonal, to get the diagonal number of the new square; $(2 \times 1) + 1 = 3$, so the new square has a diagonal number of 3. If you draw the second square and measure its diagonal, the actual length is between 2 and 3, so again our figure is less than one unit away from the actual measurement—but this time, it's a little more.

Repeat the same process again. Add the side and the diagonal of the second square, to create the side of a third square: 2 + 3 = 5. Double the side of the second square and add the result to the diagonal, to create the diagonal of the third square: (2 x 2) + 3 = 7. If you draw the new square and measure the diagonal, you'll find that the diagonal of a square with a side equal to 5 has a diagonal between 7 and 8, so—as with the first square—the diagonal measure produced by Theon's method is within 1 of the actual value, but is a little less.

Repeat the same process again, adding the side and the diagonal to get the new side, and doubling the side and adding this to the diagonal to get the new diagonal. 5 + 7 = 12, and (2 x 5) + 7 = 17; the fourth square will have a side of 12 and a diagonal of 17. The actual length of the diagonal falls between 16 and 17, so here again, as with the second square, the diagonal number is a little more than the actual value.

The same operation can be repeated again and again, making ever larger squares, with diagonal numbers that are always within 1 of the actual measure of the diagonal, and alternating between being a little above the correct figure and a little below it. (This is where the term alternation comes from.) If we treat the values of the sides and diagonals as ratios, we get a series of ratios—1:1, 2:3, 5:7, 12:17, 29:41, 70:99, and so on—which come ever closer to the actual ratio between the side and the diagonal of a square, 1:√2. These ratios quickly become very close—99/70, in decimal terms, equals 1.4142857..., while the square root of 2 works out to 1.4142135....

In this way, methods based on alternation allow the sacred geometer to work out number equivalents for relationships that can't be exactly expressed in number. Patterns similar to Theon's can be used to approximate the √3 relationship, as well as the others used in traditional sacred geometry.

Meditation for Card 22

After the usual opening process, imagine a circle. Then, as in the card, imagine two circles side by side inside the first circle; then two more inside each of the smaller circles; then two more side by side inside these. Continue until the circles have become so small that they form what looks like a straight line across the center of the original circle.

When this pattern of images is built up solidly in your mind's eye, go on to the topic of the meditation, which is the relation between perfection and imperfection in the reality we experience around us. Use the idea of alternation to explore this, and draw on any of the material we've covered above. As before, consider the topic in a general way for a time, then take one train of thought and follow it out to its end. Finish the meditation in the usual way.

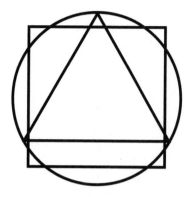

The Third Circle

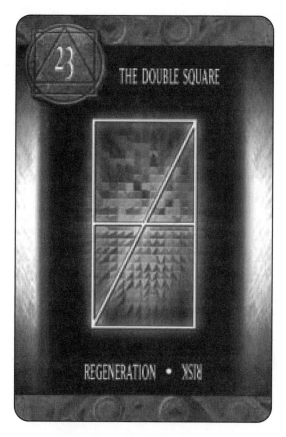

23: The Double Square

This card completes the triad of essential creative factors that are used in traditional sacred geometry. Just as the vesica piscis of Card 7 is the classic expression of the $\sqrt{3}$ relationship, and the square and diagonal of Card 20 provides the standard geometrical form of the $\sqrt{2}$, the double square with its diagonal gives us the last of the three fundamental root relationships of sacred geometry—the square root of 5, or $\sqrt{5}$.

In certain ways, the double square echoes both of the other two figures just mentioned. From one point of view, it's simply a development from the square and diagonal of Card 20; the square is joined to a second square of the same size, and the diagonal links both together. Seen from another point of view, it unites two squares the way that the vesica piscis unites two circles.

But the double square is not just another version of the relationships we've already explored. If the side of each square is equal to 1, the diagonal of the double square is equal to $\sqrt{5}$—again, a ratio that can't be expressed by any fraction or decimal figure. Where the $\sqrt{2}$ stands for generation, and the $\sqrt{3}$ for relation, the $\sqrt{5}$ represents *regeneration*, the transforming process by which a pattern transcends the limits of its own nature and opens up new potentials. In turn, it's the $\sqrt{5}$ that opens the way to the proportion known as the precious jewel of sacred geometry—the Golden Proportion, or Golden Section.

Upright Meaning: Regeneration

WHEN IT APPEARS UPRIGHT IN A READING, The Double Square suggests that the design you have made can be the basis for unimagined transformations. From its vantage, you may be able to reach new possibilities that were previously closed to you, or understand the patterns before you in unexpected ways. So that these new potentials do not slip away, attention to what is happening is called for.

IN PRACTICAL DIVINATION, this card upright means that you stand at a crossroads, facing new and unexpected possibilities. While a business-as-usual approach may still be possible, it's rarely the best choice, and may involve closing off options that lead beyond your wildest dreams. The Double Square upright calls for original thinking and a willingness to ignore old ideas about what is possible and what isn't. In some cases, this can also be a sign that a more spiritually centered approach is a good idea.

Reversed Meaning: Risk

WHEN IT APPEARS REVERSED IN A READING, The Double Square suggests that the unexpected possibilities in the design before you include dangers you haven't yet noticed. The lines and patterns before you combine in subtle ways, and some of these open up potential dangers that should not be ignored.

IN PRACTICAL DIVINATION, this card reversed means that the situation involves a significant degree of risk. Whether you realize it or not, you are in danger of losing things you value, and the more carelessly you face the situation the less likely you are to come out the other side in one piece. It's especially important not to fall into the habit of thinking that any change must be for the better. However bad the situation may seem, it could get worse, and you may wish to consider carefully before making changes you can't undo.

Exercise for Card 23

This exercise will use blank paper and the ordinary set of geometer's tools. To begin, draw a square, using either the construction from the exercise for Card 13 or the one from the exercise for Card 20. If you use the latter, draw in both of the square's diagonals once the square itself is constructed.

The goal of this exercise is to construct a second square next to the first, and of exactly the same size. Start by putting the metal point of the compass on one of the lower corners of the square, and setting the compass width to the length of the diagonal—that is, to the distance from that corner to the opposite one. Draw an arc up from the opposite corner until it's well past the midpoint of the square's upper side. Then move the metal point of the compass to the other lower corner of the square, and with the compass at the same setting, draw another arc up from the other upper corner, crossing the first arc above the middle of the upper side (see Diagram E-23).

Line up the straightedge on the point where the two arcs cross and the point where the square's two diagonals cross, and draw a line connecting these. Where this line crosses the upper side of the square, mark point A.

Next, leaving the compass at the same setting, put the metal point on each of the square's upper corners in turn and draw two arcs, of a quarter circle each, in the space above the original square. (It's not necessary for these arcs to cross each other.) Then line up the straightedge on point A and each of the original square's lower corners in turn, drawing two lines, which cross at point A and go out to intersect the two arcs you've just drawn. Where the lines cross the arcs, mark points B and C. Connect points B and C with each other, and with the upper corners of the square below, to form a new square exactly the size of the original one.

Meditation for Card 23

After the usual opening, imagine a square. Once this is built up solidly in your mind's eye, imagine a second square above the first, as in the card, and the single diagonal that connects them. Consider this image for a time, and then turn to the topic of this meditation, which is the concept of regeneration—the possibility of stepping outside existing limits by coming to see things in a new way.

As before, consider the topic in a general way for a time, then take one train of thought and follow it out to its end. Finish the meditation in the usual way.

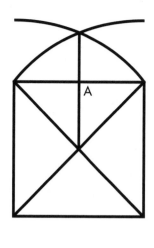

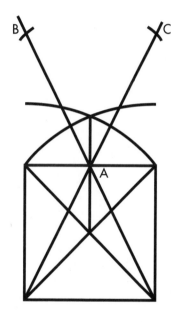

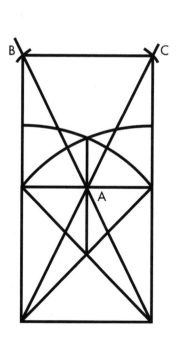

Diagram E-23

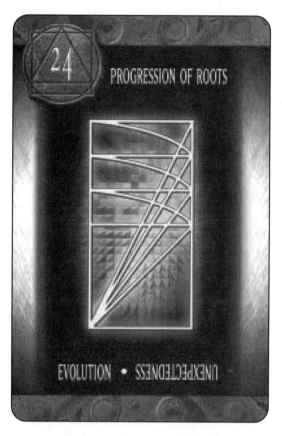

PROGRESSION OF ROOTS

EVOLUTION • UNEXPECTEDNESS

24: Progression of Roots

At this point in our progress through the cards, the diverse patterns of sacred geometry we've unfolded begin to spiral back inwards toward unity. The two approaches to practical design used in traditional sacred geometry, the ad triangulum and ad quadratim systems, were often seen as opposites with no middle ground. As the cube in Card 19 showed, though, the core relationships that define these two systems—the √3 and √2 ratios, respectively—can both be derived from the same geometrical pattern. This same point will be made with even more force by the geometrical factors at the heart of the present card.

As we saw in Card 20, Square and Diagonal, the diagonal of a square with sides equal to 1 has a length equal to √2. A square, on the other hand, is simply a special kind of rectangle—one with a length that's equal to its width. Imagine a different rectangle, one with a width of 1 and a length equal to √2. If we were to draw in the diagonal of such a rectangle, the length of the diagonal would be equal to √3.

This process can be taken even further. Imagine a third rectangle, one with a width of 1 and a length of √3. Its diagonal would be √4, which is equal to 2. As we've already seen, a rectangle with a width of 1 and a length of 2—that is, a double square—has a diagonal of √5. A rectangle with a width of 1 and a length of √5 has a diagonal of √6, and so on.

It's worth taking a few moments to think about what this implies. Starting with the simple square and diagonal, it's possible to produce all three of the prime ratios in traditional sacred geometry, one after another, by repeating the same process over and over again. The √2 and √3 relationships, in other words, aren't necessarily opposites; they can also be stages in a common process. Nor does the √5 relationship come from out of the blue to transform the opposition into a more balanced interaction; it's another stage in the same process, carried on a little further. Each relationship develops out of another and leads to another, in an unfolding current of evolution.

Upright Meaning: Evolution

WHEN IT APPEARS UPRIGHT IN A READING, Progression of Roots suggests that the design you're drawing has its own, inner patterns to unfold, whether or not these were what you had in mind. From the lines and shapes you've drawn on the tracing board, new ones will unfold, and if you let them go along with their own innate wisdom you are likely to be astonished and delighted by the results.

IN PRACTICAL DIVINATION, this card upright means that the situation has a momentum and a direction of its own, and will develop according to its own inner processes. That development may well take it in unexpected directions, and may bring together factors that you see as opposites. This is often a very good sign in divination, since it tends to mean that the situation will take care of itself if you simply let it alone.

Reversed Meaning: Unexpectedness

WHEN IT APPEARS REVERSED IN A READING, Progression of Roots suggests that the designs on the tracing board have gone beyond your ability to control them, or even to predict where they are going. The forms and lines you've drawn have developed a life of their own, and are combining and interacting in ways you can't predict and may not prefer. Still, at this point, there's actually not much you can do about it.

IN PRACTICAL DIVINATION, this card reversed means that the situation is moving in unexpected directions, and the outcome can't be predicted given the information at hand. Researchers in the field of chaos studies have pointed out that huge and utterly unpredictable consequences can spiral out from the smallest events; the flap of a butterfly's wing in Mozambique can set off a chain of events that can send a hurricane sweeping over Florida two months later. The problem in using this information, of course, is figuring out which of a billion butterflies to watch!

Exercise for Card 24

In the exercise for this card, we'll explore the pattern of progression of roots directly. Start by constructing a square, using the method from the exercise for Card 20. Using the straightedge, extend two opposite sides of the square out in the same direction, as shown in Diagram E-24; make sure you extend the lines at least far enough to allow you to draw in another square. For the sake of clarity, we'll label the corners of the square on the side where the lines don't extend as points A and B, and the corners where the lines start their extension as points C and D.

Now put the metal point of the compass on point A, and set the compass width so that the pencil point reaches to point C at the opposite corner of the square, across the diagonal. Draw an arc down from C until it crosses the extended line; mark point E here. Then move the metal point to B, set the pencil point at D, and draw an arc up from D to the extended line. Mark point F where arc and line cross. Draw a line from E to F to complete rectangle ABFE, which is a *√2 rectangle*—that is, a rectangle where the length relates to the width (or vice versa) in the ratio 1:√2.

Now put the metal point of the compass back on A, set the width to the distance from A to F, and swing an arc down from F to the extended line, marking point G where arc meets line. Move the metal point to B and repeat the process, swinging an arc from E to the line, marking point H. Draw a line from G to H to complete rectangle ABHG, which is a √3 rectangle. (If you want to doublecheck this, construct a vesica piscis with the distance from A to B as the radius of the two circles; the length of the vesica's major axis will be the same as the length of rectangle ABHG's long side.)

Now repeat the process, setting the compass width to the distance from A to H and drawing arcs from H and G to the extended lines, marking points I and J. If you've followed the instructions carefully, rectangle ABJI will be a double square. Check this by setting the compass width to AB, putting the metal point at D, and drawing a semicircle from A through C to I, showing that lines AB, AD, CD, and DI are all the same length.

If you wish, you can extend this further, creating √5, √6, √7, and higher rectangles. These saw little use in traditional sacred geometry, but they have some interesting properties and may be worth further exploration.

Meditation for Card 24

After the usual opening process, imagine a square. Exactly as in the exercise for this card, imagine the square unfolding into a √2 rectangle, a √3 rectangle, and a double square with its diagonal. Then turn your

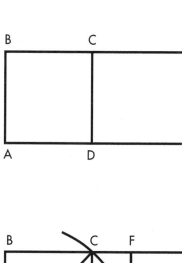

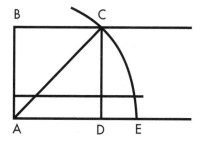

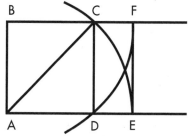

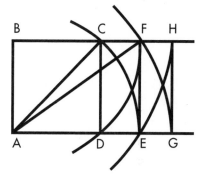

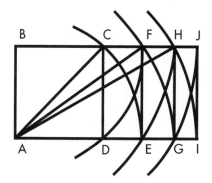

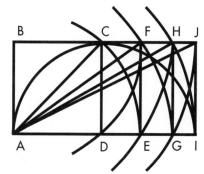

Diagram E-24

attention to the topic of this meditation, which is the way these three factors proceed from one another. Think about the different meanings we've discussed for these three root-relationships, and try to see how generation gives rise to relation, and relation to regeneration. (You may find it useful to read back over the material for Cards 7, 20, and 23 before you start.)

As before, consider the topic in a general way for a time, then take one train of thought and follow it out to its end. Finish the meditation in the usual way.

DISCONTINUOUS PROPORTION

RELATION • DEPENDENCE

25: Discontinuous Proportion

The theory of proportions is among the important mental tools of the
traditional sacred geometer. What is a proportion? Geometers draw
an important distinction between ratios, which are relationships between two measures, and proportions, which are *common relationships linking two or more different ratios*. Let's see how this works.
Imagine that you have two numbers—for instance, 1 and 2. The relationship between them is a ratio: the ratio of 1 to 2, or 1:2 in mathematical shorthand.

Now let's say you have four numbers—1, 2, 3, and 6—paired up in some way, so that 1 is paired with 2 and 3 with 6. (Perhaps they are the lengths of lines in a drawing, or parts of a building.) You know that the first pair relate to each other in a 1:2 ratio. If you examine the second pair, you notice that they relate to each other in the same way—6 is twice as large as 3, just as 2 is twice as large as 1. In the language of proportions, 1 is to 2 as 3 is to 6, or in shorthand 1:2::3:6.

This relationship is known as a *discontinuous proportion*. (It's "discontinuous" because there doesn't have to be any particular relationship between the two pairs of numbers—the second pair could as well be 11,624:23,248, and the proportion would still hold.) Sacred geometers use proportions of this sort to make sure that different patterns, even on very different scales, all relate to the same meaningful ratios.

Upright Meaning: Relation

WHEN IT APPEARS UPRIGHT IN A READING, Discontinuous Proportion suggests that the patterns before you are connected to others, which you may or may not see just now. Between the lines and forms that you've drawn and these others, there may be any number of different kinds of connections, but the link is there and can be followed up if you give attention to it.

IN PRACTICAL DIVINATION, this card upright means that the situation facing you right now has connections to other forces or factors that aren't so obvious. This may be a good time to open your eyes and ears wide, and pay attention to the things going on around you, even if they don't seem to be related to the situation that concerns you most. When Discontinuous Proportion appears upright, it often means that something apparently small and unimportant is actually the key to the entire puzzle.

Reversed Meaning: Dependence

WHEN IT APPEARS REVERSED IN A READING, Discontinuous Proportion suggests that you have drawn the design before you in such a way that someone else is going to have to complete it for you. You have made your patterns dependent on someone else's contribution, and now you will have to see if that is going to come your way—or not.

IN PRACTICAL DIVINATION, this card reversed usually means that you are depending on someone else for something that, under other circumstances, you might just as well have done yourself. In some ways, this card reversed is the opposite of Card 18, which points toward situations in which you actually need help. Here and now, you are waiting for someone else to do your work or carry your burden for you, and as a result you will have to deal with the very mixed benefits of dependency.

Exercise for Card 25

As the exercise for this card, we'll be exploring a process that was once among the most common and useful tools of the practicing sacred geometer. It's called "finding the fourth proportional," and not all that long ago it used to be part of a basic education in math all over the Western world.

What is a fourth proportional? Imagine for a moment that you only had three of the numbers in the example we used earlier in this section. You have 1 and 2, and you know that the first term of the second pair of numbers is 3 . . . but you don't have the last number. That number is called the fourth proportional.

Working out the fourth proportional in numbers can be done, but it's not always the best approach. If the measurements that you're using happen to be in whole numbers, as in the example just given, you're in luck; you can solve problems like this easily by using simple algebra. If the measurements work out to complicated fractions or, worse still, to irrational numbers like $\sqrt{2}$, you have a lot more work ahead of you. If you use geometry, on the other hand, the process is simple no matter how difficult the numbers may be.

For this exercise you'll want to use graph paper, as it lets you get past the details of construction into the actual process more quickly, and it also allows you to check your work by arithmetic if you want to. (If you've mastered the constructions used in the cards we've covered up to this point, you can do it on unlined paper; give it a shot if you're feeling confident.) Your geometer's tools are the only other things you'll need.

Start by drawing three lines, all of different lengths, over by one side of the paper. These are your three measurements. Mark them with the letters W, X, and Y. The fourth proportional, the measurement you are trying to find, will be Z.

Now draw another line, at least as long as lines W and Y put together, along the middle of the paper. Use your straightedge, and line it up with one of the lines of the graph paper for convenience. Then mark three points, A, B, and C, on the line. A can go anywhere convenient, but should be close to one end of the line. The other two points are placed by measuring: the distance between A and B is the same as the length of line W, and the distance between B and C is the same as the length of line Y. (You can do this by setting the width of the compass points equal to the length of the line, putting the metal point on a point you've already established, and drawing a small arc across the line to show where the other point belongs.)

Then draw a second line, at right angles to the first one, up from point A. (You can construct a right angle geometrically if you wish, or you can simply follow the graph lines.) On this second line, mark point D, so that the distance from A to D is equal to the length of line X. You now have all three of your measurements mapped onto the construction (see Diagram E-25).

At this point, all you have to do is draw another line at right angles to the first line, starting at point C and going the other direction. Then line up the straightedge on points D and B, and draw a line from D through B to intersect the third line. Mark point E where

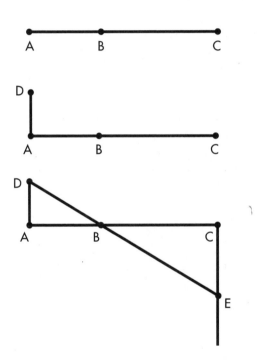

Diagram E-25

these two lines intersect. The distance from C to E is the length of the fourth proportional, line Z, which is related to Y in the same ratio as X is to W.

Meditation for Card 25

After the usual opening process, imagine any simple geometric figure you wish. Build it up solidly in your mind's eye. Then imagine it becoming first larger, then smaller, in such a way that it keeps exactly the same shape, and every part stays in the same relationship to every other part.

Once you have imagined this clearly, turn to the topic of the meditation, which is the relation between change and stability. See what the image has to say to the experiences you've had in life of things that change, and of things that don't seem to change. As before, consider the topic in a general way for a time, then take one train of thought and follow it out to its end. Finish the meditation in the usual way.

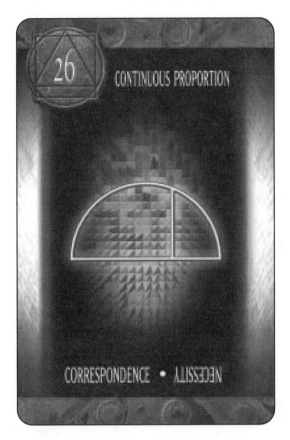

26: Continuous Proportion

Card 25, Discontinuous Proportion, introduced the basic idea of proportion and explored it through examples and exercises. As you may remember, a proportion is a relationship linking two or more different ratios—for example, the double proportion found in ratios such as 1:2, 3:6, and 121,874:243,748. In a discontinuous proportion, the measurements making up the different ratios have no particular connection with each other besides the proportion itself.

In a continuous proportion, things are a little different. Here, *the second measurement of the first ratio is the same as the first measurement of the second ratio.* Put another way, a continuous proportion involves not four terms, like a discontinuous one, but three; the first term relates to the second in the same way that the second relates to the third. For example, the numbers 1, 2, and 4 form a continuous proportion. Two is the double of one, and four is the double of two; in shorthand, 1:2::2:4, "one is to two as two is to four."

Continuous proportions are among the most useful of all the tools in the sacred geometer's kit. The relation that binds together 1, 2, and 4 can be extended further, of course, including 8, 16, 32, and so on. The same is true of subtler, more complex continuous proportions. These appear constantly in architecture and design based on the principles of sacred geometry, and create a powerful sense of internal harmony and balance. In a building planned and built according to such proportions, everything corresponds to everything else, forming a harmony of the eye as beautiful as any music. This experience is related to the ancient concept of *correspondence*—the idea that everything in the universe is connected to everything else, that "thou canst not touch a flower without troubling of a star."

Upright Meaning: Correspondence

WHEN IT APPEARS UPRIGHT IN A READING, Continuous Proportion suggests that the lines and forms in the design before you are linked by exact patterns of correspondence. Each change you make in the design, even in its smallest part, will have influences all across the tracing board. This calls for caution, but it also opens up extraordinary possibilities.

IN PRACTICAL DIVINATION, this card upright means that the situation is very delicately balanced, and any action you take, any change you make, will affect everything else. The patterns you set in motion aren't random or capricious; they will be precise reflections of what you do, how you do it, and what your motives are. This has obvious links to the concept of karma—the idea that what you get out of life depends on what you give—and issues of karma may be more than usually important in your life at this time.

Reversed Meaning: Necessity

WHEN IT APPEARS REVERSED IN A READING, Continuous Proportion suggests that the lines and forms on the tracing board are linked solidly together by relationships that are beyond your power to change. Like it or not, what you see is what you get; the patterns before you will continue to unfold with all the relentless precision of a mathematical equation, and there isn't much you can do about it at this point.

IN PRACTICAL DIVINATION, this card reversed means that the situation is what it is, and for the time being, at least, you will have to live with it. Not everything in life is open to negotiation or change! In many cases, this card is a warning that you don't have as much influence as you think, or that you're expecting the world to conform to your ideas, rather than developing your ideas on the basis of your experience of the world. This can be a recipe for disaster; you can convince yourself that cars don't exist, and learn not to notice them when they drive by, but if you go for a walk across the freeway you can still be run over by what you don't see.

Exercise for Card 26

The method of finding the fourth proportional, which was taught in the exercise for Card 25, is one of several useful geometric skills that used to be common knowledge among most people with a basic education. The subject of this exercise is another. It's a method of finding the geometrical mean, and it once saw constant use by artists, architects, designers, and other practitioners of sacred geometry.

What is a geometrical mean? The word *mean* means "middle," and a mean between two numbers is simply a middle number that relates the two together in some meaningful way. There are various kinds of means. The geometrical mean is another way of talking about the middle term in a continuous proportion where the ratio between the first two terms is the same as that between the last two. In our example above, 1:2::2:4, 2 is the middle term of the proportion, and it can also be described as the geometrical mean between 1 and 4.

This is an easy example, since it involves nothing but whole numbers and a simple proportion. Things can get much more complex when you're working with relationships like √3 or the Golden Proportion. Trying to deal with these by way of numbers is difficult at best. Again, though, geometry offers an easier way.

For this exercise, graph paper is recommended; the exercise can be done on unlined paper, but graph paper will make it easier for you to check your work. Start by drawing, along one side, two lines of any length you like; for the sake of convenience, one should be a good deal larger than the other, and each one should be an exact number of graph-paper squares in length. (It can be any number of squares you like—14, 9, 33, or whatever—but it shouldn't be 15 and part of a sixteenth, for instance.) Mark the lines as line 1 and line 2.

Now draw a line across the middle of the paper, lining up your straightedge on the grid lines of the graph paper. Mark three points on this line—A, B, and C. The distance from point A to point B should be equal to the length of line 1, and the distance from B to C should be the length of line 2. (Use your compass to measure the distance exactly.) Now, from point B, draw another line at right angles to the original line, and extend it until it's as long as the longer of your two lines.

The next step is to find the center of the whole distance from A to C. You can do this with the construction from the exercise for Card 10, or simply "cheat" by counting graph-paper squares. Once you've found and marked the center, put the metal point of the compass there, set the compass width so that the pencil point comes to A, and draw a semicircle around to C, cutting through the other line (the one at right angles to AC) in the process.

Where the semicircle cuts the other line, mark point D (see Diagram E-26). Line BD will be the geometrical mean between line AB and line BC, so that AB, BD, and BC form a continuous proportion.

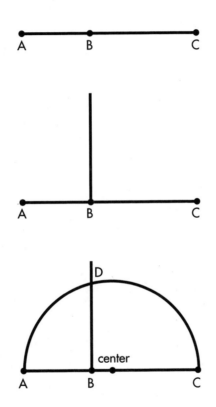

Diagram E-26

Meditation for Card 26

After the usual opening, imagine a simple geometrical shape—a square, a triangle, a circle, or what have you. Build it up solidly in your mind's eye. Then imagine yourself moving closer to it, and discovering that it is made up of smaller versions of the same shape, clustering together. You come closer and closer, and the smaller shapes prove to be made of even smaller ones, themselves made of still smaller ones, and so on, as far as your imagination will reach.

Turn to the topic of the meditation, which is the concept of interrelation. A common theme of spiritual teachings from around the world is that all things are interconnected. Think about this, and in particular about situations in your own life where interconnections show themselves. As before, consider the topic in a general way for a time, then take one train of thought and follow it out to its end. Finish the meditation in the usual way.

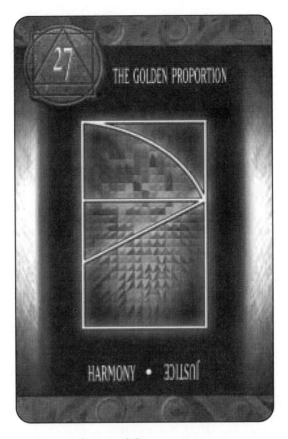

27: The Golden Proportion

The idea of proportion—a relationship linking two or more different ratios—has been introduced and discussed earlier in our exploration of the Oracle. The two kinds of proportion we've examined, though, don't exhaust the possibilities that this branch of sacred geometry has to offer. Along with discontinuous proportions and continuous proportions is a third, very special kind of proportion, which might be called a hypercontinuous proportion. This is the precious jewel of sacred geometry, the Golden Section, or Golden Proportion.

As you've already learned, a discontinuous proportion is a relation between four different measures, which we can label a, b, c, and d, such that a:b::c:d. A continuous proportion relates three measures, a, b, and c, such that a:b::b:c. How can this be taken any further? Simply by making c equal to the sum of a plus b. Then we have a:b::b:(a+b).

Now it so happens that there's only one ratio in all the universe that will make this equation work, and it involves yet another irrational number. This number is signified by the Greek letter phi, Φ. In approximate numbers, it works out to around 1.61803398875 . . . (and so on for an infinite number of digits) but—like π or the square roots of 2, 3, and 5—it can't be expressed exactly by any fraction or decimal number. On the other hand, like these others, it *can* be expressed exactly by geometry.

Φ is a number with astonishing properties. Not only does it make the special "hypercontinuous" proportion, or Golden Proportion— 1:Φ::Φ:(1+Φ) works out exactly—but adding 1 to Φ gives you Φ^2, and subtracting 1 from it gives you the fraction ⅟Φ! Entire books have been written about the ways that Φ dances around itself in mathematical terms, and books have also been written about the ways that Φ and the Golden Proportion appear over and over again in the natural world. The spiral of seeds in the head of a sunflower is based on the Golden Proportion; so are the curves of a nautilus shell, the lengths of the bones in your fingers, and many other relationships.

Researchers have found that of all shapes, those based on the Golden Proportion seem most balanced and beautiful to the human eye. Clearly, Φ is a geometrical symbol of harmony and beauty, but the deep internal harmony of the Golden Proportion has its more challenging side as well.

Upright Meaning: Harmony

WHEN IT APPEARS UPRIGHT IN A READING, The Golden Proportion suggests that the design you have drawn has achieved the rare quality of inner harmony. It relates to itself, and to the world around it, with harmony, consistency, and beauty. This is a time to sit back and contemplate a job well done.

IN PRACTICAL DIVINATION, this card upright means success, pure and simple, with no drawbacks or limitations whatsoever. This is one of the best omens in the Oracle; it means that you have done, are doing, or are planning to do the right thing at the right time in the right situation, and the results will unfold from that in perfect harmony.

Reversed Meaning: Justice

WHEN IT APPEARS REVERSED IN A READING, The Golden Proportion suggests that the designs you have drawn on your tracing board have been weighed in the balance and found wanting. Perhaps you haven't paid attention to the materials that were to be used, or the purpose for which they were meant, or the rules of design or building; in any case, there's no helping it, and you will need to start over from the beginning.

IN PRACTICAL DIVINATION, this card reversed means that you, and no one else, have made the situation exactly what it is. What is happening to you is not the fault of circumstances, other people, or random chance; it's the precise and mathematical result of your own thoughts, words, and deeds, and you will have to live with it. The concept of karma is relevant here. This may not be much consolation, but if you pay attention to the lessons involved, you may be able to avoid going through the same thing again in the future.

Exercise for Card 27

This exercise will teach another basic construction that was once common knowledge among educated people. The basic Golden Rectangle, with short sides equal to 1 and long sides equal to Φ, is an essential part of the old traditions of design using sacred geometry. Like the other irrational numbers used in the traditional lore, it's surprisingly easy to construct.

Start by drawing a square, using either of the two constructions introduced so far (in the exercises for Cards 13 and 20). The next step is to divide it in half. One easy way to do this is to construct a vesica, using the two ends of one side of the square as the centers of the circles, and the length of the side as the circles' radius; line up the straightedge on the points of the vesica, and draw the major axis of the vesica, extending it as needed so that it goes through both sides of the square. Mark points A and B where the line intersects the sides of the square.

You now have a square divided into two long rectangles, and if you're paying attention, you've noticed that each of these rectangles is a double square. (Their long sides, after all, are twice the length of their short ones.) Next, put the metal point of the compass on point A and adjust the width until the pencil point is on the opposite corner of one of the rectangles; swing an arc upwards through a quarter-circle or so. Move the metal point to B, and swing a second arc up in the same way.

Line the straightedge up on the sides of the original square, and extend the sides up until they intersect the arcs. Where the arcs and lines cross, mark points C and D. Draw in line CD to complete a new rectangle above the square (see Diagram E-27).

This new rectangle is a Golden Rectangle . . . and so is the rectangle formed by adding the new rectangle to the square! These two rectangles relate to each other, furthermore, by the Golden Proportion; the ratio between the short side of the new rectangle to the side of the square is 1:Φ, and so is the ratio between the side of the square and the side of the combined rectangle, which is made by adding the rectangle's short side to the side of the square—again, a:b::b:(a+b).

If you add another, larger square, with a side equal to the side of the original square plus the short side of the new rectangle, the much larger rectangle formed by the two squares and the rectangle will also be a Golden Rectangle. Similarly, if you take the new rectangle and cut it into a square as wide as the rectangle's short side and another, leftover rectangle, the leftover rectangle will be another Golden Rectangle.

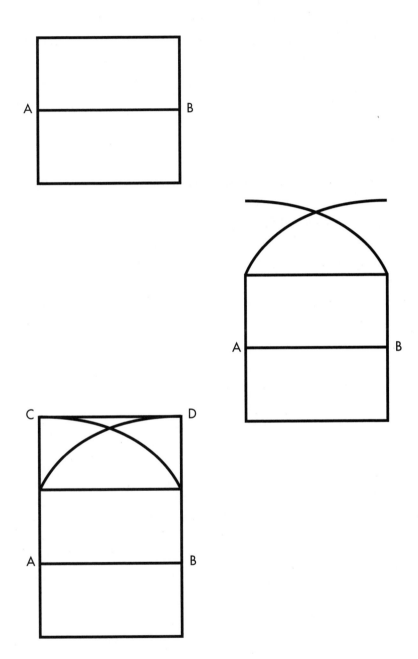

Diagram E-27

Once you have the basic ratio in place, it's possible to keep on turning out an endless sequence of Golden Rectangles, all of them in perfect proportion to each other, by simply adding or subtracting squares. The Golden Proportion is like that.

Meditation for Card 27

After the usual opening process, imagine the Golden Rectangle shown on the card; leave out the lines and arc inside the rectangle, and just try to pay attention to the overall shape. Consider it, turning it over in your mind and trying to feel how the sides relate to one another. When this is clearly built up in your imagination, turn to the topic of the meditation, which is the idea of beauty. What is beauty? What do we mean when we say that something is beautiful? Is beauty just a matter of perception by the senses, or is there something else involved?

As before, consider the topic in a general way for a time, then take one train of thought and follow it out to its end. Finish the meditation in the usual way.

THE PENTAGRAM

POWER • RESPONSIBILITY

28: The Pentagram

From the Golden Proportion unfolds one of the most important and most controversial symbols in traditional sacred geometry. The pentagram is one of the same family of geometrical patterns as the hexagram, the octagram, and the dodecagram, all of which we've already examined. Unlike these others, it has developed a very strange reputation. The emblem of wizards, pagans, and mystics of a wide array of traditions, the pentagram is feared by some people, revered by others, and ignored by very few.

One factor in the pentagram's meaning that is not often recognized is its connection to the Golden Proportion. Ratios and continuous proportions based on Φ run all through the pentagram's geometries. Consider Diagram A-28. The ratio between the lengths of line BC and line AB is Φ; so is the ratio between AB and AC; so is the ratio between AC and AD.

Caught up in the pentagram's interwoven lines, as well, is the entire question of magic—the ancient art of using the subtle powers of consciousness to reshape the universe of human experience. Though it's had a very checkered reputation in recent centuries, there's nothing especially spooky or evil about magic; it's simply a part of human potential. In what we patronizingly call "primitive" societies, it's an everyday part of life, woven into every moment of every day. It's only in more "advanced" cultures that people get far enough from their own experience to lose track of the dance of magical forces all around them.

Magic is the primal form of power, and all other kinds of power—political, economic, social, spiritual—echo the imagery and myths of magic in one way or another. (Think about the way that people in modern America treat money; is it any different from the way that people in tribal societies treat magical amulets?) For our present purposes, the pentagram can stand for all forms of power, and challenges the sacred geometer to face the ancient questions of ability and responsibility that power always invokes.

Upright Meaning: Power

WHEN IT APPEARS UPRIGHT IN A READING, The Pentagram suggests that the drawing you have made on the tracing board is, in some sense, a magical talisman. It has the capacity to summon power of one kind or another. If you take the time to learn how to make it work and to direct the power it evokes, countless possibilities open up before you.

IN PRACTICAL DIVINATION, this card upright means that power is available to you in the situation, if you choose to make use of it.

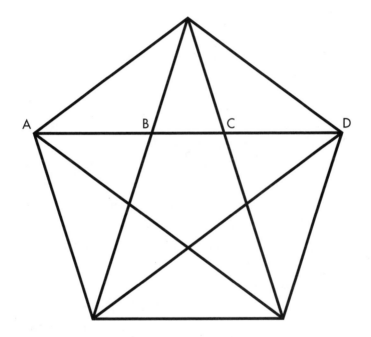

Diagram A-28

This is very often a positive sign, for it means that you have the power you need to achieve what you want. It also implies, however, that if the situation needs fixing, you're the one who is in a position to fix it; this is not a good time to wait for someone else's help!

Reversed Meaning: Responsibility

WHEN IT APPEARS REVERSED IN A READING, The Pentagram suggests that you need to remember that no one else's hand is holding the pen upon your tracing board, nor will anyone else be responsible for the patterns you draw there. Those patterns may not be as abstract or as playful as you assume; you may end up having to live with the results of your designs, and so may other people.

IN PRACTICAL DIVINATION, this card reversed means that you need to keep in mind that power brings responsibility with it, and your actions may have consequences and implications for which you will be held responsible, one way or another, further on down the road. At its harshest, The Pentagram reversed can have some of the same quality of implacable justice as The Golden Proportion reversed, but more often it simply reminds you that what you do is important, and not just in the present moment.

Exercise for Card 28

For this exercise, the construction of a regular pentagram, start with the method for the quadrature of the circle given in the exercise for Card 11. You'll only need to use three of the four points where the cross intersects the circle's circumference—the two ends of the horizontal line, and the upper end of the vertical one. For our present purposes, we'll call the first two points A and B, and the last point C.

Now set the compass to the same setting it was at when you drew the original circle; put the metal point on B, and draw an arc through the center of the circle, swinging it out until it crosses the circumference on both ends and forms a vesica piscis (see Diagram E-28). At

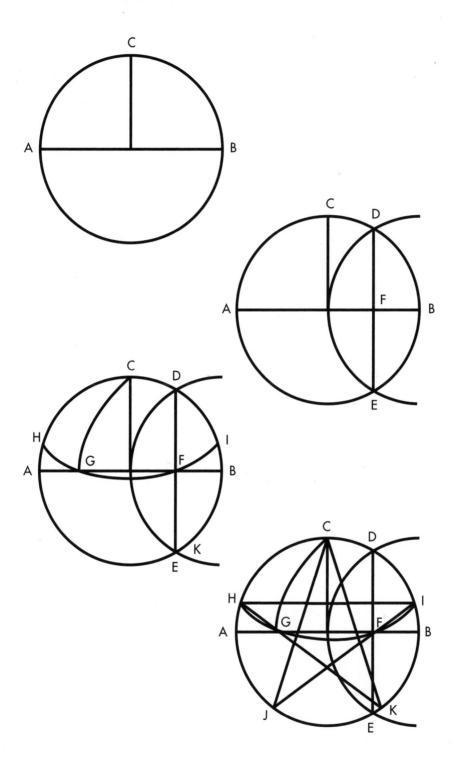

Diagram E-28

the ends of the vesica's major axis, where the arc and the circle intersect, mark points D and E. Line up the straightedge on these points and draw line DE. Where DE intersects line AB, mark point F.

Put the metal point of the compass on point F and change the compass width until the pencil point comes exactly to point C, up at the top of the circle. From C, draw an arc down until it crosses line AB, and mark point G at the intersection.

Next, move the metal point of the compass to point C, and change the compass width to the distance from C to G. Swing an arc out to either side to the circumference, and mark points H and I. With the metal point on H and the compass setting the same, mark point J further down the circumference; with the metal point on I, do the same thing, marking point K.

Finally, draw in lines CJ, JI, IH, HK, and KC to complete your pentagram.

Meditation for Card 28

After the usual opening process, imagine a circle. Then, tracing one line at a time, imagine a pentagram taking shape inside the circle. When this image has been built up solidly in your mind's eye, go on to the topic of the meditation, which is the idea of power. Explore what power means to you, what you would do if you had it . . . and why it is that you think that you *don't* have it.

As before, consider the topic in a general way for a time, then take one train of thought and follow it out to its end. Finish the meditation in the usual way.

THE DODECAHEDRON

TRANSCENDENCE • NOITATUMSNART

29: The Dodecahedron

The dodecahedron is the last of the five Platonic solids. Made of pentagons, it shares the same pattern of Golden Proportion relationships we saw in the last card, The Pentagram. Like the other Platonic solids, it relates to one of the elements of ancient science, philosophy, and magic. The tetrahedron, octahedron, icosahedron, and cube connect to the four material elements—fire, air, water, and earth, respectively—but the dodecahedron corresponds to the fifth element, the element of spirit.

There's a lot of confusion over the concept of spirit these days—not surprising, really, in a culture based on ways of thinking that deny that spirit exists at all! The word originally meant "breath," and comes from a root that also shows up in words like "re*spir*ation." From the idea of breath, it came to be used for the subtle life-energies that are related to breath, and then for a whole range of realities that go beyond the purely physical. Since most people in the Western world know very little about the nonphysical levels of being, it's no wonder that it's come to be used rather loosely.

For our present purposes, the complex geography of the realms of spirit isn't crucial. The one point that needs to be kept in mind, and gets forgotten far too often, is that spirit isn't simply a vague, formless "something" onto which we can project our own desires and fantasies. According to the seers and mystics of all times and cultures, it's the world of matter that's comparatively formless and vague, and the world of spirit that's intricate, powerful, and structured. To borrow a metaphor from C. S. Lewis, we tend to think of the spiritual side of reality as some vague mist steaming upward, when a better image might be strong, skilled hands reaching down from above to shape and transform.

Upright Meaning: Transcendence

WHEN IT APPEARS UPRIGHT IN A READING, The Dodecahedron suggests that the design on your tracing board has become a framework for energies descending from the spiritual levels of being. In ancient thought, a temple was understood as a vessel for spiritual presences; in this sense, the plan you have drawn outlines a temple, and subtle powers are beginning to set the curtains shimmering and the incense aswirl.

IN PRACTICAL DIVINATION, this card upright means that the situation is being shaped by spiritual influences. Where Card 28 upright is like a magical talisman, The Dodecahedron suggests a temple or a shrine, one in which the divinity is very much present and active! Whether you understand what is happening or not, this is a good time to try to move along with it, rather than trying to pursue your own idea of what should happen.

Reversed Meaning: Transmutation

WHEN IT APPEARS REVERSED IN A READING, The Dodecahedron suggests that the design you have drawn is an image of yourself, and as that design changes, you must change along with it. It may be that spiritual powers are guiding your pen, or that you yourself are beginning to recognize the ways in which you need to bring greater balance, harmony, and creativity to bear in the lines and forms of your own self.

IN PRACTICAL DIVINATION, this card reversed means that what the situation is demanding of you is inner change. This is perhaps the most frightening part of any spiritual journey, and it's an important reason why so many people either ignore the spiritual altogether or put up some comfortable imitation in its place. The tangle of compromises, evasions, and half-truths that makes up the ordinary human personality has to give way to something stronger, clearer, and more honest before it can open itself to the spiritual realm—or, really, to any aspect of life. This is the work ahead of you at this time.

Exercise for Card 29

This exercise, like those for the other Platonic solids, will require a craft knife or a good pair of scissors as well as the usual geometer's tools, and it's useful to do it on heavier paper than usual; you'll need two sheets this time, as well. This is the most difficult construction you'll be given in this book, but if you follow it step by step you shouldn't have any trouble.

The first step in this construction is to draw a regular pentagon, which you can do by following the instructions for the exercise for Card 28, except for the last step of drawing in the pentagram itself. As you start, make sure that the original circle is small enough that you can fit another circle of the same size next to it without running off the edge of the paper. Instead of the final step, draw in lines CH, HJ, JK, KI, and IC to form the pentagon (see Diagram E-29). You may find it useful to make these lines darker than usual, so that they stand out among the others.

Then set the compass to the radius that you used to make the original circle. Put the metal point on each of the five corners of the pentagon in turn, and draw a circle around each corner. Ignore the part of the circle inside the pentagon. (In fact, you don't even have to draw it.) On the outside, the circles intersect at five points. Mark these as points L, M, N, O, and P. Now, without changing the compass setting at all, draw five more circles with the five points you've just marked as the centers. These five new circles will become the framework for five new pentagons.

Next, set the compass to the distance between points C and H— that is, to the length of the side of your original pentagon. Put the metal point of the compass on each of the corners of the pentagon, and draw short arcs to mark in the corners of the new pentagons. (I won't give letters to each of these new points, since we'd quickly run out of alphabet! Simply mark these in the same way you did in the exercise for Card 28.) Draw in lines to create the five pentagons around the original one.

When you've done all that, you're halfway there. What you have to do next is to repeat the same process exactly, with the same measurements, on another piece of paper. Once you have two clusters of six pentagons each, cut the clusters out—cut along four sides of each of the outside pentagons, but don't cut them apart from the central one, or you'll have wasted all that effort—bend the outside pentagons up until their edges meet, and tape them together. Finally, join the two halves of the dodecahedron together—the points on each half go into the spaces between the points on the other—and tape. Take the time to study your dodecahedron from various angles, and see the patterns it forms.

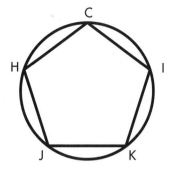

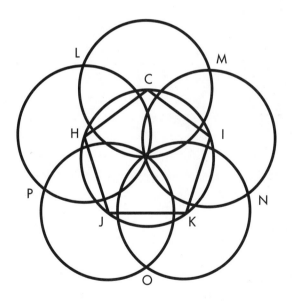

Diagram E-29, continued on page 183

Meditation for Card 29

Start with the usual opening process, and then imagine a pentagon. Once you have it solidly built up in the mind's eye, add another, and another and another, until you have formed the same sort of rosette of six pentagons you made in the exercise. Then imagine the outer pentagons folding back, away from you, to meet and form a half-dodecahedron. All at once, become aware that there is another half behind it, unseen, completing the dodecahedron.

Once this imagery is solidly established, go on to the topic of the meditation, which is the idea of spirit. Think of what this means to you, how it relates to the world of your experience, and how it relates to the patterns of the four elements—the patterns you explored in your meditations on Cards 16, 17, 18, and 19. As before, consider the topic in a general way for a time, then take one train of thought and follow it out to its end. Finish the meditation in the usual way.

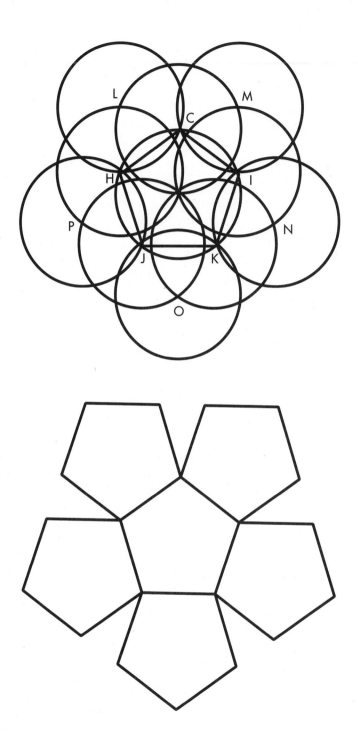

Diagram E-29, continued

30: Unity of Primary Roots

As we continue the process of spiralling back in toward the unity that underlies all the patterns of sacred geometry, new relationships become apparent. In examining Card 24, Progression of Roots, we discovered one of the ways in which the three central root relationships of the art—the √2, √3, and √5 ratios—unfold out of a single process. In this card, in turn, we'll be seeing how it's possible to start from any of the three and unfold the other two, in perfect proportion.

The lesson that this construction has to teach isn't limited to the realm of sacred geometry. It's a common turn of phrase that opposites attract, and you may have seen this (or experienced it yourself) in human relationships, or in other aspects of life. The truth underlying the cliché is that every pair of opposites is part of a greater unity. Hot and cold are simply different kinds of temperature, male and female different expressions of a common humanity, life and death different stages in a single process.

This recognition of the underlying unity in all oppositions can bridge the gap that seems to open up so often in ordinary life, where opposites sometimes seem to hedge us around on all sides. At the same time, it's a door into paradox, into realms that we may not be able to understand within the limits of our ordinary habits of thinking and experiencing.

Upright Meaning: Reconciliation

WHEN IT APPEARS UPRIGHT IN A READING, Unity of Primary Roots suggests that even though there appears to be conflict and opposition among the patterns on your tracing board, you will be able to draw the different lines and forms back together again into unity. Subtle connections link together even those things that seem most at odds with one another, and if you can find these or sense them, you can use them to reconcile the different factors of your design.

IN PRACTICAL DIVINATION, this card upright means that conflict, division, or disagreement in the situation can be resolved in a constructive way. It often means that different factions or individuals, who seem to be moving in opposite directions, are actually carrying out different parts of a larger pattern, and can be brought together in a constructive way if this is done gently and perceptively. It can also mean that no conflict will arise in the first place.

Reversed Meaning: Paradox

WHEN IT APPEARS REVERSED IN A READING, Unity of Primary Roots suggests that the design on your tracing board has taken shape according to principles that may not make sense to you. Lines and forms are combining and interacting in ways you hadn't expected and can't predict, and the overall design seems to be turning into something other than what you had in mind.

IN PRACTICAL DIVINATION, this card reversed usually means that the situation is taking shape in ways that seem paradoxical or confusing. Things you thought were going one way turn out to be headed in a completely different direction, and your actions produce results you didn't anticipate. This can be a difficult experience, especially for those who like their lives predictable, but it's important to remember that finite minds facing an infinite universe are going to find themselves in this sort of situation now and again.

Exercise for Card 30

The exercise for this card involves a simple construction that allows any one of the three fundamental root relationships to unfold into the other two. The resulting diagram is an important one, for it sums up many of the principles of traditional sacred geometry in a single image. You'll need your ordinary geometer's tools, and several sheets of unlined paper.

There are three ways to start—with a square, with two circles forming a vesica piscis, or with a double square. We'll take these one at a time.

To start from a square, begin by constructing a square, using either of the constructions we've studied so far (the exercises for Cards 13 and 20 give these). Draw in the diagonal of the square. Choose one side of the square, and label the two corners on that side points A and B; the two on the opposite side are points C and D.

Set the compass to the distance from A to B, and draw two circles, one with A as center, the other as B, creating the vesica piscis. Draw a line between the two points where the circles cross, dividing line AB in half at point E.

Next, draw a line from point C through point E, and extend it up until it crosses the circumference of one of the circles at point F. Draw another from D through E, and extend it to cross the circumference of the other circle at point G. Draw lines AF, FG, and GB to create the second square ABGF, completing the figure (see page 189).

To start from a vesica piscis, begin by drawing a vesica according to the construction given in the exercise for Card 7. Make the centers of the two circles points A and B. Draw in the major and minor axes of the vesica, and mark point C where they cross. Now put the metal point of the compass on point C, and set the compass width to the distance from C to A. Draw a circle around C, which should pass through both A and B. Where the circle cuts the major axis of the vesica, mark points D and E.

Then draw four lines—from A to D, from A to E, from B to D, and from B to E—extending each of these out to intersect the circumference of one or the other of the two circles. Mark points F, G, H, and I where these lines cross the circles. Draw in lines FG, GH, HI, and IF to create both the square and the double square, and draw in line FH to complete the diagram.

To start from a double square, start by constructing a double square as shown in the exercise for Card 23. Then simply draw in the diagonal of the lower of the two squares, to give you the √2 relationship, and draw in two circles with their centers at the midpoints of the two long sides, and the compass set to the length of the short side, to give you the √3. Draw in the major axis of the vesica piscis to complete the diagram (see page 191).

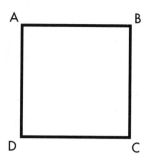

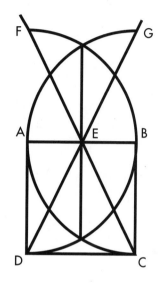

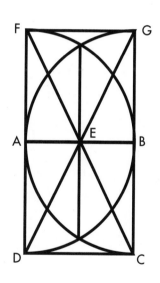

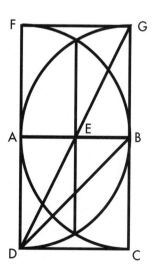

Diagram E-30, from a square

Meditation for Card 30

After the usual opening process, build up, in your mind's eye, the diagram shown on the card. Try to imagine it as clearly and exactly as possible, and see how the square, the vesica, and the double square interact. When you've established this pattern of imagery firmly in your imagination, turn your attention to the topic of the meditation, which is the links among the three root relationships—$\sqrt{2}$, $\sqrt{3}$, and $\sqrt{5}$—and the three corresponding principles of generation, relation, and regeneration.

As before, consider the topic in a general way for a time, then take one train of thought and follow it out to its end. Finish the meditation in the usual way.

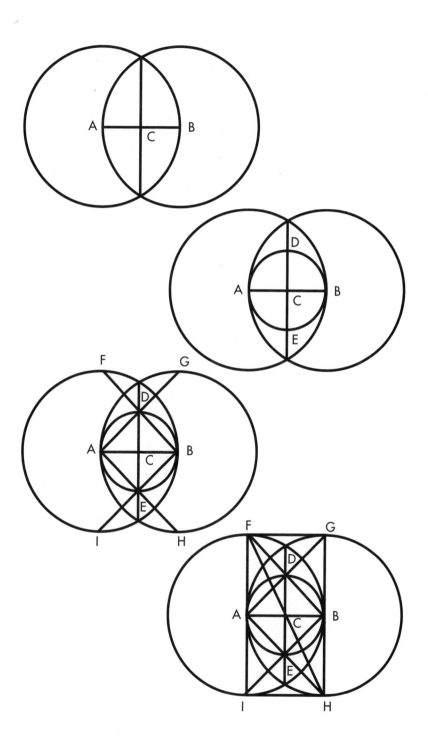

Diagram E-30, from a vesica piscis

31: The Sphere

Along with the five Platonic solids discussed earlier—the tetrahedron of fire, the octahedron of air, the icosahedron of water, the cube of earth, and the dodecahedron of spirit—a sixth figure has long played an important part in the traditions of sacred geometry, and of the other ancient sciences of number. This is the sphere, the projection of the circle into three dimensions.

The geometry of the sphere is relatively complicated, and spherical constructions were among the last things added to the symbolic toolkit of traditional sacred geometry. (This is why domes—which can't be designed without a mastery of spherical geometry—didn't come into common use in the ancient world until Roman times.) Still, even in far more ancient times, the sphere and its properties were studied by wise people, for it was clear even then that the sphere was the dominant shape in the universe surrounding the Earth.

There's a common modern notion that claims no one knew that the Earth was round until the mariners of the Age of Exploration sailed around it, but this just shows how little people actually know about the life of the mind in ancient times. The correct shape of the Earth was certainly known to the ancient Greeks by the fourth century B.C.E., and there's good reason to think it may have been figured out much earlier. The philosopher Eratosthenes of Cyrene even calculated the Earth's size in the third century B.C.E., and came within a few percent of the modern figure. As for the contemporaries of Columbus, the textbook of astronomy used in university courses all over Europe in 1492—John of Sacrobosco's *On The Sphere*—starts out with a set of good logical proofs that the Earth is round. (The debates between Columbus and his critics had to do with the size of the Earth, not its shape. His opponents argued that the distance from Spain to the Indies was farther than any fifteenth-century ship could travel—and they were right! It's just that no one imagined there might be two unknown continents in the way.)

With the sphere, then, we are dealing with the symbolic image of the cosmos itself. The sun, the moon, the planets, and the Earth itself are spheres, and this led philosophers of an earlier age to suggest that the universe itself might be shaped the same way. This ancient idea has received startling modern support from Einstein's theory of relativity, which holds that space itself is curved and that the entire universe is spherical.

Upright Meaning: Infinity

WHEN IT APPEARS UPRIGHT IN A READING, The Sphere suggests that the design you have drawn on your tracing board leads out endlessly in all directions, like a map with edges that border on the unknown. The possibilities that are open to you right now are limitless, for all practical purposes, although it's worth remembering that the longest journey around the surface of a sphere is the one that eventually leads you home again.

In practical divination, this card upright means that the possibilities before you are greater than you have any way of imagining. This is often an extremely positive sign in divination, although it can mean that you're getting into something much bigger than you think. In some ways, the message of The Sphere upright is like that of Card 1, The Unmarked Card, for there's a common theme of limitlessness. Where The Unmarked Card is simply undefined, though, The Sphere leads out into limitless realities that have already taken shape, and only wait for your arrival.

Reversed Meaning: Unknowability

When it appears reversed in a reading, The Sphere suggests that the design on your tracing board has passed beyond your understanding. The lines and forms you have traced interact with others you can't see at all, producing patterns and relationships you can't predict and may not even see, and the final shape of the design you're drawing is completely hidden from you.

In practical divination, this card reversed usually means that one or more of the major factors at work in the situation are completely outside your picture of the matter. In some ways, this card is a more intense form of Card 30 reversed, but what you're up against here is not simply a matter of paradox—it's a complete failure to grasp what's going on. It may be that you don't have the knowledge or the experience to figure out what is happening, it may be that your basic assumptions are so far off the mark that you don't have a clue about the actual factors at work, or it may simply be that the situation is so complex and delicate that its outcome can't be predicted at all.

Exercise for Card 31

The Sphere is the one card in the Sacred Geometry Oracle for which there's no practical geometrical exercise. The reason for this is simple: there is no way to construct a sphere, or even a really close approximation to one, using the tools of the sacred geometer and a sheet of paper. A sphere can have no angles and no flat surfaces; only a pattern with an infinite number of infinitely small sides would do the job—and this is a little hard to carry out in practice!

To explore the sphere, it's necessary to stray out of the boundaries of sacred geometry itself just a little, and venture into another branch of the ancient quadrivium—the fourth branch, astronomy. One good way to do this is to go outside on a clear evening just after sunset, when the moon is in its first quarter and one or more planets will be visible. (You can look this up in any good almanac.) Find a grassy slope with a good view of the western sky, and lie down on your back, looking out into infinite space. Though the sun is below the horizon, you can see its rays streaming upwards from the west, and the crescent of the moon shows that those same rays are illuminating one face of our sister world. If Venus or Mercury are visible, be aware of the sun's rays lighting them also.

As you gaze into the sky, then, try to become aware—not just as an intellectual idea, but as an actual experience—that you are on a sphere yourself, spinning through the same heavens as the sun and its other planets. Try to realize, with your whole being, that you are looking out rather than up—that the Earth is not a flat surface beneath you but a sphere among spheres, sweeping through space as it turns on its axis—that the sun and moon are not setting, but rather that the part of the Earth you're on is turning away from them.

It's a dizzying experience, and you may not want to try to drive immediately afterwards.

Meditation for Card 31

After the usual opening process, imagine a sphere taking shape around you, extending perhaps a yard or so out from you. Try to build up the image of the sphere surrounding you as solidly as possible in your mind's eye. When you've done this, imagine the sphere getting slowly bigger, expanding to surround the room, your home, your neighborhood, your state or province, your country, your continent, your planet. Allow it to keep getting steadily bigger, until it contains the whole universe. Then release the image.

At this point, turn your attention to the topic of this meditation, which is the idea of the universe itself. The word "universe" comes from the Latin *universus*, "that which turns as one." Think about this, and about the things you know or believe about the universe that surrounds you. As before, consider the topic in a general way for a time, then take one train of thought and follow it out to its end. Finish the meditation in the usual way.

32: Squaring the Circle

The magnum opus of sacred geometry, the supreme goal of countless generations of effort, was the process known as "squaring the circle"— that is, producing a square and a circle that had either exactly the same area, or exactly the same distance around the outer edge. This may seem trivial at first glance, but it actually deals with issues that go straight to the core of traditional sacred geometry.

The square is a very easy figure to calculate with. If you want to know the distance around its outer perimeter, all you have to do is measure one side and multiply by four; if you want to know its area, you simply need to measure one side and multiply the measurement by itself—that is, square it. There's no ambiguity or difficulty involved.

The circle, by contrast, is a very difficult figure indeed to calculate with, because the ratio between the diameter of a circle and its circumference is π, pi, the most famous of all irrational numbers. Since π can never be expressed precisely by numbers, you can know exactly either the diameter or the circumference of a circle, but never both—and this raises a barrier to squaring the circle that no amount of ingenuity can breach.

In fact, mathematicians proved long ago that *there is no way to square the circle exactly by geometrical methods.* It simply can't be done. This doesn't mean, however, that the attempt is not worth making. Many of the classic methods for carrying out an approximate squaring of the circle are accurate to within a tiny fraction of the total measurements involved, and they also have lessons of their own to teach.

In traditional sacred geometry, the circle is often used as a symbol of the realm of spirit, while the square represents the world of our everyday lives as perceived by our five ordinary senses. To try to reconcile these two, to bring spirit down into matter or to raise matter up into spirit, is the central work of mystical and magical traditions worldwide.

Upright Meaning: Attainment

WHEN IT APPEARS UPRIGHT IN A READING, Squaring the Circle suggests that the diagram on your tracing board has achieved its goals as completely as anything can. You have squared the circle, brought heaven and earth into harmony, and achieved as much perfection as it is possible to manage in the world of human experience. At the same time, the diagram is finished, and your task now is to set it aside and move on.

IN PRACTICAL DIVINATION, this card upright means success, pure and simple. There is no better sign in the Oracle. Whatever the situation may be, and whatever the obstacles may have been, the goals you have been seeking and the dreams you have tried to make real are on your doorstep. It's time to celebrate—but it's also time to prepare for the next phase of your life.

Reversed Meaning: Impossibility

WHEN IT APPEARS REVERSED IN A READING, Squaring the Circle suggests that the design you are trying to draw on your tracing board simply can't be done, and that is that. Despite all your efforts and skill, you are not going to achieve what you want to achieve. Like it or not, it's time to take a deep breath, wipe the tracing board clean, and start again from the beginning.

IN PRACTICAL DIVINATION, this card reversed means that your goals and dreams in this situation are not within your reach. No matter how hard you try, no matter how clever you are, no matter how much you think you deserve to get what you want, it's not going to happen, and you need to deal with that fact. Courage and persistence are valuable traits, but it's also worth keeping in mind that pounding your head against a brick wall hurts you and doesn't do anything to the wall.

Exercise for Card 32

There are various traditional methods for squaring the circle to within a few percent of the exact value. The method we'll be using here is among the simpler, and it also has the useful feature of starting on ground we've already covered several times. This particular construction is an ancient one, and has been explored in detail by the modern sacred geometer John Michell.

Begin by marking a point, point A, and drawing a circle of any convenient size around it. Choose a second point, point B, on the circumference of the circle, and draw a circle of the same size around it, creating a vesica piscis. Then draw a line from A to B, extending it out to both sides to touch the circumferences of the circles on either side. Mark points C and D where the circles cross, and points E and F where line AB touches the circumferences.

Next, put the metal point of the compass on E, set the width to the distance from E to F, and draw an arc up and down from point F through at least a third of a circle. Move the metal point to F, and swing an identical arc up and down from E to intersect with the first arc, forming a larger vesica. Mark points G and H where the two arcs cross.

Then draw lines from E and F to H. Where these two lines cross the original circles, mark points I and J. Lining up the straightedge on points I, D, and J, draw a line across the larger vesica out to the arcs on either side. Where this new line touches the arcs, mark points K and L.

If you now construct a square with line KL as its base, using the construction from the exercise for Card 20, and draw a circle with C as center and the distance from C to D as radius, you've accomplished one form of squaring the circle—the perimeter of the square will be nearly equal to the circumference of the circle. This diagram has another mystery to reveal, though. If you draw lines from point C to points K and L, the resulting triangle has exactly the same proportions and angles as a vertical section through the Great Pyramid of Giza (see Diagram E-32). Several modern students of sacred geometry have suggested that this, in fact, is one of the secrets hidden the structure of the enigmatic Egyptian monument.

Meditation for Card 32

After the usual opening process, imagine a circle in the midst of endless space. Once this is built up solidly in your mind's eye, imagine a square below it. The square and the circle are the same relative sizes as the ones in the card. After a time, imagine the square rising and the circle lowering, until they overlap exactly.

Then turn your attention to the topic of the meditation, which is the relation between spirit and matter. Just as many different forms

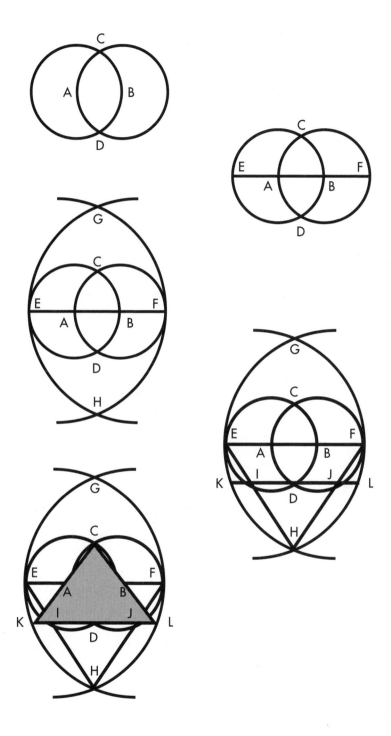

Diagram E-32, producing the proportions of the Great Pyramid of Giza

and functions in sacred geometry are used in different methods of squaring the circle, so a great deal of the material we've covered elsewhere in this book has relevance here.

As before, consider the topic in a general way for a time, then take one train of thought and follow it out to its end. Finish the meditation in the usual way.

THE HUMAN CANON

UNITY • DIVERSITY

33: The Human Canon

The teachings of sacred geometry may seem very abstract at first glance, and indeed it's traditional to present them in an abstract way to beginners in the art. Points and lines, circles and squares, and the unfolding of the basic root relationships form a world of their own—one that seems much simpler than the complicated and muddy reality we encounter in the rest of our lives.

Still, the separation between geometry and everyday reality is an illusion. On an obvious level, of course, the patterns of sacred geometry traditionally took shape in the beautiful and moving structures of ancient architecture, just as the lifeless geometries of profit and efficiency produce the ugliness of so much in the way of modern design and construction.

But the connection between geometry and the universe of our experience goes a good deal deeper. Our own bodies, the instruments through which we experience the world, are structured by geometrical principles. If you fall close to the human average, the distance from your head to your navel relates to the distance from your navel to the floor in the Golden Proportion, and the distance from your navel to the floor relates to your total height in the same ratio. Many similar proportions and ratios structure every part of the human body.

Equally, as countless experiments have shown, people find shapes based on the Golden Proportion more attractive than any other, and they find shapes based on any meaningful geometrical pattern more attractive than those simply put together at random. What this shows is that geometry is as deeply rooted in our minds as it is in our bodies.

In ancient times, considerations like these led the masters of sacred geometry to build their art around what is called the *human canon*. (The word "canon" is an old term for "standard" or "rule.") This was simply the principle that the measures, relationships, and patterns used in sacred geometry were drawn from the human body itself. From ancient times through the Renaissance, the same proportions that relate the fingers to the hand and the limbs to the body also related the parts of a building to the whole shape of the structure, and the structure itself to the surrounding landscape. The result was a built environment that was not only stunningly beautiful, but that also made it easier for the people living in and around them to live lives of the same sort of proportion and balance. All these are things that would be well worth reviving in the present world.

Upright Meaning: Unity

WHEN IT APPEARS UPRIGHT IN A READING, The Human Canon suggests that the design you have sketched out on your tracing board is, ultimately, a picture of yourself. All the proportions and relationships you've used have unfolded from within you, and the unity that governs the whole pattern is one that you yourself have put there, whether you realize it or not.

IN PRACTICAL DIVINATION, this card upright means that there is a fundamental unity at work in the situation, and it derives from you. If you are encountering the same kind of situation over and over again, you may want to try to figure out how you yourself might be causing it—and if you don't like it, you may want to think about ways of changing yourself so that you don't call it into being again. More broadly, this card upright is a reminder that you are the most powerful force shaping the universe of your own experience, and you need to seek in yourself the means of reshaping that universe closer to your heart's desire.

Reversed Meaning: Diversity

WHEN IT APPEARS REVERSED IN A READING, The Human Canon suggests that the design on your tracing board contains more factors and patterns than you have imagined, and more potentials for new creation than anyone can ever grasp. No matter how simple the design is, or how complex it has become, the possibility always exists that you will come up with something that no one has ever drawn before.

IN PRACTICAL DIVINATION, this card reversed means that you may not be paying enough attention to the real diversities that are present in the situation. While it may look just the same as other situations you've seen in the past, it has features of its own that you're not noticing. This card reversed serves as a reminder that the universe is more complex and diverse than any of our belief systems or mental models can really grasp, and that it's always possible for things to happen that have never happened before.

Exercise for Card 33

For this exercise, you'll need the ordinary set of geometer's tools, several sheets of paper, and one other thing—your own body. (You may also find a mirror useful at some points.) There isn't a specific construction involved; rather, your goal is to explore some of the geometries of yourself.

The hand and the face are perhaps the easiest parts of the body to work with, since they are around the same size as the geometrical diagrams with which you've been working. Start by drawing four lines, to represent the fingers, and using the compass to mark off distances equal to the length of the different joints of your fingers. See how the different measures relate to one another. Try making different constructions with one or another measurement as basis—triangles, vesicas, squares with their diagonals, Golden Proportion rectangles, and so on.

Now do the same thing with your face, using a mirror to guide your hand, and being especially careful near the eyes. When your eyes are open to their normal width, how close do they come to perfect vesicas? What are the proportions of your nose, your mouth, your forehead, the line of your jaw? Take these explorations as far as you wish, and be aware that this sort of measurement and calculation was an important part of the training of a sacred geometer in ancient times.

Meditation for Card 33

After the usual opening process, imagine a circle and a square, as in the last exercise, but already overlapping, as in the artwork on Card 33. When this image has been built up solidly in your mind's eye, imagine yourself in the center of the diagram. You should picture yourself naked, and try to make the image as exact as possible. If you don't have a very good idea of what you look like with your clothes off, a few minutes of privacy before the meditation in a room with a full-length mirror should solve the problem.

When this whole pattern of imagery is firmly established, turn your attention to the topic of the meditation, which is—yourself! Think

about who and what you are; try to get past simple verbal labels—
"I am a woman," "I am a man," "I am thin," "I am fat," "I am (fill in the
blank)"—toward something deeper and less arbitrary, founded not on
words but on experience. Who are you? What are you? Let the questions turn over in your mind, and seek a sense of your own nature. Go
on as long as it seems productive, then finish the meditation in the
usual way.

Reading the Oracle

The thirty-three cards of the Sacred Geometry Oracle form an alphabet of symbols that can be used for divination, as well as for other purposes, such as meditation or study. An alphabet, though, is only the first step of the way we form and communicate meaning. In ordinary language, we put letters of the alphabet together to form words, sentences, and entire texts. In the subtle language of divination, similarly, we put one or more cards together with a diviner, a querent—the person for whom the divination is done, who may or may not be the same person as the diviner—and a question or situation on which the reading will shed light.

There are many different ways to approach the process of divination. One useful way divides it into three different stages: first, preparation; second, casting the reading; and third, interpretation. We'll take these one at a time.

Preparing for the Reading

Different people approach the process of divination in different ways. Some people prefer a formal, ritualized process to help them enter into the state of heightened awareness and intuition that makes divination possible. Others find that such things simply get in the way, and prefer to plunge straight into the divining process. One way or another, though, it's important to still the ordinary chatter of the mind, and to focus your awareness on the work you are about to do.

Divination isn't a game, and it should be treated with a certain degree of seriousness. As the word itself suggests, it's a matter of raising the awareness up above the everyday human level, and coming into closer contact with the divine consciousness that shapes all things.

While being pompous or pretentious about it is hardly productive, it's useful to set the process of divination a little apart from the activities and concerns of ordinary life.

It's also important to prepare for the reading in other ways. One of these is to formulate the questions to be answered or the situation to be clarified in a way that will help the divination make sense. The other is to make sure that the cards themselves are ready to respond to the questions. Each of these has its own requirements.

Preparing the Questions

In many systems of divination, the standard approach is to have the querent (and sometimes the diviner as well) choose a single question that the reading will answer. It's entirely possible to approach the Sacred Geometry Oracle in this way, and if you've previously used any other card-based divination system you will have little trouble in figuring out how this can be done. The specific focus of this Oracle, though, is on a somewhat different approach—one that's often more flexible and more informative than the usual, more highly structured approach.

We'll cover the details of this method a little further on, when we discuss casting and interpreting the reading. In preparing for this method, though, it's important to be sure you understand the question or situation that the divination is going to explore. If you're doing a reading for another person, you'll need to work with the querent to open up the different issues and factors involved, asking questions and encouraging the querent to talk about his or her concerns, hopes, fears, and needs in the situation. If you're doing a reading for yourself, the same process will need to go on inside your own head.

This part of the divination process has much in common with the sort of work that counselors and clergy do. Patience, tact, and the ability to listen are of central importance here. Particularly crucial is the habit of keeping an open mind, and avoiding any judgment in advance of the divination process itself. See what the cards have to say before you jump to any conclusions about what is going on!

In the course of exploring the question or situation, you should keep a mental list of the important people, forces, and factors that are involved; feel free to discuss the list with the querent, and make sure that you agree about what the important factors are. You'll need to have these in mind when it comes to the actual divination process. Three to eight factors will give you a good place to start; more than that can be difficult to keep straight in the first stage of divination, although they can be added in later.

Preparing the Cards

Once you have finished exploring the question, you need to prepare the cards. This is done by clearing the deck, a simple process that rearranges all the cards and makes sure that they don't stick together during shuffling. It's done by dealing the cards out one at a time, facedown, into three piles: the first card to the first pile, the second to the second pile, the third to the third pile, the fourth to the first pile, and so on. When all the cards in the deck have been dealt out into the three piles, put the first pile on top of the second one, then the combined pile on top of the third, forming a single pack to be cut, shuffled, and dealt in the divining process itself.

Preparing Yourself

There is also the matter of readying yourself for the divination, and entering into a state of consciousness that will foster the divining process instead of interfering with it. One simple ceremonial method that helps to do this, and falls somewhere in the middle of the extremes mentioned above, goes as follows.

First, spend a moment or two stilling your mind, and then take your cards out of the box and hold the deck in your hands, facedown, so that the diagram on the back is visible.

Second, imagine the diagram expanding out from the back of the topmost card until you (and the querent, if you're divining for someone else) are sitting in the center, surrounded by a triangle, square, and circle formed of lines of pure light. Hold this image, allowing it to build up solidly in your mind's eye.

Third, say, either out loud or silently in your mind, the following words:

> Let the circle of spirit and the square of matter come into harmony here and now; let wisdom take shape and knowledge be shown, and the form of hidden things be revealed.

This concludes the ceremony, and the process of preparation. At this point, you're ready to begin the divination itself.

Casting the Reading

One of the reasons that card-based divination systems have become so popular in recent years is that the process of casting the reading is so much simpler with cards than with most other methods. Astrology demands either a solid knowledge of mathematics or a certain amount of skill with computer programs; geomancy, though much simpler, still requires the diviner to learn the precise set of steps needed to unfold a geomantic chart from sixteen lines of points; even the I Ching, done in the traditional way with yarrow stalks, needs a fair amount of practice to get the somewhat complicated process to come out right.

By contrast, anyone who knows how to play solitaire already has all the necessary skills to cast a reading using a card-based system. All that's necessary is that the deck be shuffled thoroughly while the diviner thinks intently of the question to be answered. The deck is then cut, and the cards uncovered by the cut are dealt off, one at a time, and read.

In many card-based divination systems, it's standard to have a set of fixed spreads, with different positions that have specific meanings in the context of the reading as a whole. As mentioned above, it's entirely possible to do this with the Sacred Geometry Oracle. Still, our focus here will be on a different way of doing readings, one that has more in common with the way that geometrical patterns themselves unfold in practice.

Once you're ready to begin the divination, then, shuffle the cards thoroughly, cut the deck, and deal out one card for each of the important people, forces, and factors in the situation about which you're divining. Start with a card for the querent himself or herself, and then deal out the others one at a time, saying aloud what each card represents. You can place them in a straight line if you wish, or arrange them around the working surface in ways that help represent their meaning to you.

At this point, begin interpreting the cards, following the guidelines given in the next section. This doesn't mark the end of the shuffling and dealing process, though! By the time you've finished interpreting this first phase of the reading, either you or the querent (or both) may well have questions about some other aspect of the situation. Shuffle what remains of the pack, cut, and deal out another card as a response to each question. Interpret those, and go on. The process ends only when you run out of questions; if you run out of cards and there's still obviously more to learn, you can make notes on what's already been revealed, gather up the cards, shuffle them thoroughly, and keep going.

Interpreting the Reading

Once you've laid out the first set of cards, the focus of the divination process shifts from the mechanics of shuffling and dealing to the subtler realm of meanings, interpretations, and intuitions—the realm where divination stops being a mechanical process and turns into a source of insight and realization. For many people, this is the difficult part of divination. Still, it doesn't have to be that way!

Very often, the great obstacle in the way of effective divination is the idea that each symbol in the divinatory alphabet has one and only one meaning. In fact, the symbols of a divination system are (or at least should be) as many-faceted as the images of dreams. The keywords and commentaries given for each of the cards of the Sacred Geometry Oracle should be treated as a starting point for your own intuitive awareness, not as a cage around the card's possibilities of meaning.

If you're comfortable with your own intuitive abilities, you should have little trouble taking the cards of the Oracle as a springboard for your own perceptions. If you've absorbed too much of our culture's distrust of the intuitive, on the other hand, it may take you a little time and practice to learn how to do this. It often helps to look at the card you're trying to understand, and simply ask yourself, "What does this make me think of? What does this bring to mind?" Listen to the answers that surface; don't dismiss any of them out of hand. Try to see or feel how the concept expressed by the keyword might relate to the factor that the card is representing.

Much of this stage of the divination can be done as a sort of dialogue in which you, the querent (if you're doing the reading for another person), and the cards all play a role. The more open you are to questions and suggestions from the querent, and hints and responses from the cards, the better the results are likely to be.

Sample Readings

Two sample readings may help show how this process is carried out.

Sample Reading 1

The querent is an office worker who is dissatisfied with her job. One of her coworkers has approached her about a business opportunity that, he claims, will allow her to double her income within six months. He has given her a packet of literature about the program, and invited her to attend a meeting where she can ask questions and learn more about the opportunity. It sounds tempting, but the literature makes vague references to some sort of payment the querent will be expected to make up front, and she has her doubts.

In the course of discussing the situation before the reading, these are the most important factors in the querent's view of the situation:

1. Herself;

2. The coworker who made the offer;

3. The offer;

4. What she stands to gain by taking up the offer;

5. What she stands to lose by taking up the offer;

6. What she stands to lose by not taking up the offer;

7. Her best response to the offer.

The cards respond to each of these as follows:

1. Card 13, The Square reversed: Inertia. This card suggests that she has stopped moving under her own power, and may be waiting for someone else to solve her problems for her.

2. Card 1, The Unmarked Card reversed: Hiddenness. This suggests that the coworker may have information he is not sharing with the querent, or hidden motives in the situation.

3. Card 22, Alternation: Approach. This card suggests that the opportunity is moving in the right direction, but may not be exactly what she wants.

4. Card 20, Square and Diagonal reversed: Consequences. This card suggests that what the querent may gain from the offer may not be what she has in mind.

5. Card 16, The Tetrahedron: Energy. This card suggests that whatever energy she puts into the offer may well turn out to be wasted effort.

6. Card 23, The Double Square reversed: Risk. This suggests that there are risks involved, which can be avoided by not taking up the offer.

7. Card 3, The Line: Extension. This suggests that the querent's best response to the situation may be to build on skills and connections she has already established—possibly by looking for another position in the same line of work she already does, possibly by exploring other fields that use many of the same skills she's developed by way of her current work.

In the course of discussing the cards, the querent admits that she'd heard rumors that the coworker who made the offer was involved in various shady marketing schemes, and had wondered why he didn't seem to be as rich as the flyers implied he ought to be! She is more interested, though, in following up some of the cards' other suggestions. Two more factors emerge from the discussion:

Card 4

Card 8

Card 1　　Card 3　　Card 2　　Card 7

Card 5　　Card 6　　Card 9

Sample Reading 1

8. The opportunities to be found in her current line of work;

9. The opportunities to be found in related professions.

The cards respond to these as follows:

8. Card 8, The Equilateral Triangle reversed: Limitation. This card suggests that there are very few possibilities open to her in the specific line of work the querent is in, and that looking for another position in this area might be overly limiting.

9. Card 21, Gnomonic Expansion: Expansion. This card suggests that a broader approach would be more productive, and hints that the querent shouldn't be afraid to think big, and to try for what seem like unlikely possibilities.

The querent has no more questions. After a little more discussion and a cup of herbal tea, she leaves in search of a copy of the Sunday help-wanted ads.

Sample Reading 2

The querent is a young man worried about his future. He has applied to a prestigious Ivy League university for graduate school, but isn't sure his grades and test scores will get him in, and he can't see any other options ahead of him if he fails to win admission. He badly wants to be told that he'll be accepted, and doesn't want to hear about any other issues involved.

These are the most important factors in the querent's view of the situation:

1. The querent himself;

2. The university;

3. The university's response to his application.

The cards respond to these as follows:

1. Card 4, The Circle reversed: Repetition. This card suggests that the querent is going around in circles, repeating a pattern

Card 1

Card 2

Card 3

Card 4

Card 6

Card 5

Card 8

Card 7

Sample Reading 2

that he's followed many times in the past, and that it's unlikely to get him anywhere new.

2. Card 15, The Dodecagram: Completeness. This card is often an indication of success, and here it suggests that the querent sees the university as a symbol of success, as something that will bring him completeness or fill what he lacks.

3. Card 32, Squaring the Circle reversed: Impossibility. This card suggests very forcefully that the querent's application will not be successful.

The querent responds to all this by becoming angry and defensive, and then suddenly bursting into tears. The diviner gets him a box of tissues and then, by a series of gentle questions, elicits a long story of family expectations, failed rebellions, and self-defeating behaviors founded on extreme perfectionism. After the querent has finished blowing his nose and getting a little more perspective on the situation, the conversation turns to the wider situation surrounding the querent's graduate-school hopes, and new questions emerge.

At this point, another set of factors seems central to the querent:

4. His family's reaction to the failed application;

5. How he can deal effectively with this;

6. Other possibilities that are open to him;

7. How he should pursue these.

The cards are shuffled and dealt, and respond as follows:

4. Card 10, The Cross reversed: Dissension. This card suggests that different members of his family will have different reactions, and there may be a fair amount of quarreling and disagreement among them.

5. Card 3, The Line reversed: Separation. This suggests that the best way for him to deal with this is to put some distance be-

tween himself and his family—emotional and psychological distance, certainly, but possibly also physical distance as well.

6. Card 23, The Double Square: Regeneration. This card suggests that the querent stands at a crossroads, facing the possibility of a life that goes beyond his previous habits and expectations, and that he may find it useful to think long and hard about who he is and what he actually wants out of life.

7. Card 1, The Unmarked Card: Potentiality. This suggests that, ultimately, the choices are his to make. It also suggests that by making his own choices—rather than allowing them to be made for him by his family, or his own assumptions, or the baggage he's carried along with him from his past—he will best be able to respond to the present situation.

The querent considers these, and then asks another question: How can he avoid falling into the same sort of perfectionism that has made his life unhappy in the past? The cards respond as follows:

8. Card 33, The Human Canon reversed: Diversity. This card suggests that the querent needs to pay attention to the ways in which every person differs from every other person, and in particular, to the ways that his needs, interests, desires, and values are different from those of the people around him. Rather than trying to judge everyone (including himself) by a single standard, he may find it more useful to recognize that each person has a unique role to play in the universe.

The querent comments that the reading has given him a lot to think about. After a little further conversation, he leaves, saying that he'll call to let the diviner know how things turn out.

A Sacred Geometry Bibliography

Sacred geometry is one of the most neglected branches of the Western inner traditions, as mentioned earlier, and the total number of worthwhile books on the subject in English today would fit on a very small shelf. Fortunately, some of the books on that shelf count as classics by any definition. Those books I would recommend to the beginning or intermediate student of sacred geometry are included here.

The following works form a basic library on the subject, one that can take the attentive student far beyond the elementary material covered in this book. Those who are interested in learning more about sacred geometry will find them to be useful guides.

Critchlow, Keith. *Order in Space* (London: Thames & Hudson, 1969).

———. *Time Stands Still* (London: Gordon Fraser, 1979).

Doczi, Gyîrgi. *The Power of Limits: Proportional Harmonies in Nature, Art, and Architecture* (Boston, Mass.: Shambhala, 1981).

Ghyka, Matila. *The Geometry of Art and Life* (New York, N.Y.: Dover, 1977).

Hambidge, Jay. *The Elements of Dynamic Symmetry* (New York, N.Y.: Dover, 1967).

Lawlor, Robert. *Sacred Geometry: Principles and Practice* (London: Thames & Hudson, 1982).

Michell, John. *The Dimensions of Paradise* (San Francisco: Harper & Row, 1988).

———. *The New View Over Atlantis* (New York, N.Y.: Thames & Hudson, 1983).

Schwaller de Lubicz, R. A. *The Egyptian Miracle* (Rochester, Vt.: Inner Traditions International, 1983).

———. *The Temple of Man* (Rochester, Vt.: Inner Traditions International, 1999).

Vitruvius Pollio, Marcus. *The Ten Books on Architecture* (New York, N.Y.: Dover, 1960).

Glossary

Air: one of the five elements of ancient philosophy, science, and magic, related to the gaseous state of matter/energy.

Alternation: a traditional process of approximating irrational numbers, which functions by creating ratios that are successively above and below the irrational number by an ever-diminishing amount.

Arc: a portion of a circle.

Circle: a set of points, all of which are the same distance from a common point (which is called the center).

Circumference: the outer edge of a circle.

Continuous Proportion: a proportion relating three measures, in which the first measure relates to the second as the second relates to the third, a:b::b:c.

Diameter: any straight line that passes through the center of a circle and touches the circumference of the circle on each end.

Discontinuous Proportion: a proportion relating three measures, in which the first relates to the second as the second relates to the third, a:b::c:d.

Earth: one of the five elements of ancient philosophy, science, and magic, related to the solid state of matter/energy.

Element: in ancient science, philosophy, and magic, one of five basic principles of existence.

Equilateral Triangle: a triangle with three sides of identical length.

Fire: one of the five elements of ancient philosophy, science, and magic, related to the radiant state of matter/energy.

Gnomon: a shape that, when added to some other shape, makes a third of the same form but a larger size.

Golden Section: *see* Golden Proportion.

Golden Proportion: a continuous proportion in which the first measure is to the second as the second is to the sum of both, a:b::b:(a+b), which can only be achieved with the irrational number Φ. The Golden Proportion is also known as the Golden Section.

Irrational Number: a number that cannot be expressed exactly as a fraction or a decimal expression.

Isosceles Triangle: a triangle with two sides of the same length, and one side of a different length.

Line: pure length, without any width.

Line Segment: the part of a line between two defined points.

Major Axis: in a vesica piscis, the line connecting the two points formed by the crossing of the circles making up the vesica.

Minor Axis: in a vesica piscis, the line connecting the centers of the two circles making up the vesica.

Perimeter: the outer edge of a shape made up of straight lines.

Pi: a number, approximately 3.14159, represented by the figure π, which is the ratio between the circumference and diameter of a circle; an important irrational number in sacred geometry.

Platonic Solids: the five regular three-dimensional figures—tetrahedron, octahedron, icosahedron, square, and dodecahedron—used in traditional sacred geometry.

Point: pure location, without any divisible parts.

Proportion: a relationship between two or more ratios.

Radius: the distance between the center of a circle and its circumference; also, a line with a length equal to that distance.

Ratio: a relationship between two measures.

Regular: having all sides and angles equal.

Right Triangle: a triangle in which one of the three angles is a right angle, that is, an angle of ninety degrees.

Sacred Geometry: the ancient tradition of geometry as a way of spiritual insight.

Scalene Triangle: a triangle in which all three sides are of different lengths.

Spirit: one of the five elements of ancient philosophy, science, and magic, related to the space-time continuum in which matter/ energy exists.

Squaring the Circle: the "great work" of traditional sacred geometry, which consists of constructing a square and a circle that have either identical perimeters or identical areas.

Vesica Piscis: (Latin, "vessel of the fish") a geometrical diagram made from two circles, each one with its center on the other's circumference.

Water: one of the five elements of ancient philosophy, science, and magic, related to the liquid state of matter/energy.

Index